D0195875

Homeworking Women

Homeworking Women

Gender, Racism and Class at Work

Annie Phizacklea and Carol Wolkowitz

SAGE Publications
London • Thousand Oaks • New Delhi

© Annie Phizacklea and Carol Wolkowitz 1995

First published 1995

All rights reserved. No part of this publication may be reproduced, stored in a retrieval system, transmitted or utilized in any form or by any means, electronic, mechanical, photocopying, recording or otherwise, without permission in writing from the Publishers.

SAGE Publications Ltd
6 Bonhill Street
London EC2A 4PU

SAGE Publications Inc
2455 Teller Road
Thousand Oaks, California 91320

SAGE Publications India Pvt Ltd
32, M-Block Market
Greater Kailash – I
New Delhi 110 048

British Library Cataloguing in Publication data

A catalogue record for this book is available from the British Library.

ISBN 0 8039 8873 7
ISBN 0 8039 8874 5 (pbk)

Library of Congress catalog card number 94-069830

Typeset by Mayhew Typesetting, Rhayader, Powys
Printed in Great Britain by Biddles Ltd, Guildford, Surrey

Contents

List of Tables

Acknowledgements

There are many organizations and individuals whose assistance in researching and producing this book was essential and whose help we wish to acknowledge. All our research was wholly funded by the Economic and Social Research Council and we wish to thank them for their support. Vera Hyare, who is an officer in the Economic Development Unit of Coventry City Council, collaborated in the planning of the survey in Coventry, carried out many of the interviews and continues to share with us some of her knowledge of homeworking in Coventry. For our success in contacting homeworkers we are indebted to the editorial staff of *Prima* magazine and members of the Working Mothers Association. We want to thank Robin Chater for his help in contacting firms. We are indebted to the firms and local authorities who participated in the research and to the many homeworkers who gave up their precious time to talk to us or to complete the postal questionnaire. Keith Halstead, Director, and Margaret Armitage, Pauline Bates and Wendy Murray of Computing Services at the University of Warwick were an enormous help. We also acknowledge the support of the Sociology Department at Warwick. Finally we thank our families, Steve, Ben, Martyn and Tim, for their forbearance.

1 | Homeworking and Women's Employment Trends

Many sociologists of differing ideological persuasions have regarded the diffusion of new technology into the home as one of the potentially liberating developments of so-called post-Fordist, post-industrial society (for example Bell, 1973; Gorz, 1985; Lyotard, 1984; Toffler, 1981). For instance, André Gorz (1985: 88) writes in *Paths to Paradise*:

> So local production for local tastes and needs becomes possible again. Better still, thanks to teletext and computers, the majority of white collar jobs and an extensive range of industrial jobs can be transferred to the employee's home and performed without any timetable constraint. Diversified and enriched these jobs can become group activities; for a family, for a group of neighbours etc.

In 1988 the Henley Forecasting Centre predicted that two and a half million people could be working at home by 1992 with the supposed benefits of the 'electronic cottage' stretching from savings in fuel and pollution reduction to the supposed benefits of the reintegration of home and work. In short, the emphasis on 'teleworking' (originally a term used to describe electronic home-based work but which now covers other flexible working arrangements such as satellite offices) has given us a rather glamorous, post-industrial image of home-based working which simply does not tally with the evidence collected over the years by the Low Pay Unit, by academic researchers and local homeworking officers and campaigns on the incidence and persistence of extremely low paid, arduous, manufacturing home-based work (for instance, Allen and Wolkowitz, 1987a; Anthias, 1983; Bagilhole, 1985; Bisset and Huws, 1985; Brown, 1974; Crine, 1979; Garrett, 1984; Greater Manchester Low Pay Unit, 1986; Mitter, 1986a, b; Phizacklea, 1990; Rai and Sheikh, 1989; West Yorkshire Homeworking Group, 1990; Wolverhampton Homeworkers Research Project, 1984; and the annual reports of Leicester and Greenwich Homeworking Campaigns). What we have, therefore, are two very contrasting and extreme images of homework. What we hope to show in this book is that homework in Britain today reflects all types of work carried out by women in the external labour market as well as the different experiences and material circumstances of women in a racialized and class-divided society. We will start by putting homework within the context of women's employment in advanced industrial societies, focusing afterwards on the particular situation in Britain.

Throughout the world the 1980s saw a continuing rise in women's paid employment set against a significant decline in full-time male jobs. Behind this overall tendency, Acker (1992) and Reskin and Padavic (1994) cite at least four distinct but related trends affecting the structure of women's employment in all advanced industrial societies. First, restructuring of employment occurred initially in manufacturing, leading to a relative decline in the better-paid, male-dominated sectors of manufacturing production. This affected the proportion of economically active men in all industrial societies. Whereas in the 1970s and for most of the 1980s it seemed that women workers in the burgeoning service sector were protected from job loss, this is no longer the case. In the United States and the UK, for instance, restructuring of clerical work is now extensive, with job cuts in banking, sales, technical and administrative support. In addition, the very recent trend to flatten managerial hierarchies is reducing what had become widened opportunities for women to move up the line through promotions or to displace men at lower levels of management. Therefore, previous trends which allowed women to move out of domestic labour and factory employment into clerical and managerial work and public services have altered, leaving many women in dead-end jobs.

Secondly, these commentators note a polarization in skill demands, in which women's jobs are increasingly divided between routine low-wage, highly controlled work and non-routine, relatively autonomous higher-waged jobs. This polarization is partly explained by the decline in skilled manufacturing jobs, which leaves former industrial workers chasing and competing for low-level service jobs, such as cleaning, which require no formal qualifications. But it is also because women have benefited from the growth in professional, managerial and administrative jobs at the other end of the spectrum. Developments in information and communication technology are also affecting women's service sector jobs. What Albin and Appelbaum (1988) term the 'knowledge-information sector' is characterized by high wages and capital intensity. Some jobs in this sector are being upgraded in terms of skill by integrating previously discrete jobs into multi-task skilled clerical work. In the case of women workers this may not necessarily be recognized, nor rewarded. For instance, female banking staff are engaged in new and more complex jobs, which include previously professional tasks. In Sweden at least, such workers are reported to have received no wage increases for their added responsibility (Acker, 1992). However, other jobs are being reconstructed along more traditional Taylorist principles, being increasingly downgraded into de-skilled fragmented tasks. Developments in data entry also mean that many routine clerical jobs are vanishing altogether.

A third trend is a growth in flexible work organization. The search for lower labour and related costs is producing an expansion in the contingent labour force whose jobs lack the permanence, security or protection previously enjoyed by many or most male industrial workers. When commentators refer to the 'contingent' labour force, they are usually referring to those workers whose numbers can be expanded or reduced according to demand (Christensen, 1989: 187). There are important national differences in the forms which the growth of the contingent labour force is taking, depending on employment law in particular (Bakker, 1988; Rubery, 1988). In the United States, the proportion of part-time workers in the labour force grew from 16 to 20 per cent in the three years between 1988 and 1991 (Acker, 1992). In countries where part-time work started from a high base the rise has been more significant. Part-time work is particularly significant in The Netherlands, Denmark and Britain, where until recently many part-time workers were not covered by the same employment benefits and protection as full-timers. In France, however, where the law does not distinguish between full-time and part-time workers, enterprises are achieving labour flexibility by expanding the numbers of temporary workers and those with short, two-year contracts. In Italy, where workers in larger firms are well protected by state regulation, most of the expansion of women's employment has been in the so-called 'informal economy'. The biggest increase in contingent work is among women. In the European Union women now comprise two-fifths of the labour force, but eight out of ten part-time workers, seven out of ten family workers and five out of ten temporary workers are women (Manchester School of Management, 1994). Homeworkers whose contractual status is ambiguous are a prime example.

These trends are leading commentators to talk of the 'feminization of the labour force' (Jenson et al., 1988), which not only refers to women constituting an increased proportion of the labour force but also has other connotations. It is often used to refer to declining terms and conditions of employment, so that a larger proportion of the labour force has come to experience 'feminized' (that is, poor and insecure) conditions of work (Reskin and Padavic, 1994; Woody, 1992) in some cases through deregulation at the national level.

A fourth trend frequently cited in the US is the increasing 'diversity' of the labour force, as demographic trends project an increasing participation of women and non-white minorities as a proportion of the labour force. However, the emphasis on diversity is marginalizing the language of 'equality' and this is making it more difficult for women to demand the rights and benefits that male employees used to take for granted (at least in large enterprises) and it may also obscure the occupational segregation which continues along racial and gender lines (Liff, 1993).

The language of 'diversity' can obscure continuing inequalities in the employment situations of black and white men and women and other minority groups, as well as the ways in which they are affected by restructuring. For instance, in the US, cuts in male-dominated heavy industrial jobs have hit the employment of Afro-American men severely, making it necessary for more and more Afro-American women to become the sole family earner. At the same time increases in service sector female employment have made it possible for Afro-American women, who before the Second World War were often confined to domestic service jobs, to enter mainstream employment in the service sector, especially in day-care centres, restaurants, hospitals and commercial laundries and clerical work (Amott and Matthaei, 1991; Woody, 1992). However, although black women's earnings have increased relative to white women, black women are still segregated in relatively low-paid service sector jobs, especially in state sector health and educational services. This meant that they were particularly badly affected by the 1980s assault on welfare in America, as consumers as well as workers, and progress in clerical jobs characteristic of the 1970s and 1980s had ceased by 1991 (Acker, 1992).

In so far as Afro-American women are concentrated in routine sales or clerical work, their jobs are more likely to be automated rather than upgraded or re-skilled. However, the United States is characterized by very complex forms of occupational segregation. For instance, East Asian women in America reveal a bi-polar distribution in jobs and are affected by structural changes in the economy in different ways. The share of Chinese, Japanese and Filipina American women in managerial and professional jobs is equal to or higher than their share of the labour force. But East Asian women are also over-represented in low-paid manufacturing and family labour jobs and it is not clear whether younger generations or more recent migrants will be able to repeat the success of the upwardly mobile, partly due to changes in job opportunities and declining stability in urban neighbour-hoods as well as racism in the labour market (Amott and Matthaei, 1991).

All of these trends are evident in Britain to a greater or lesser extent, especially the rise in women's paid employ-ment set against a significant decline in full-time male jobs. The rate of part-time work in Britain is very high in comparison to other Western countries, with 50 per cent of all white women employed in part-time jobs. Many have pointed to the lack of child-care facilities (or tax allow-ances for child care) in Britain as an explanation (Dex and Shaw, 1986). Another possibility is that British women are less dependent on full-time employment for access to health care insurance, as is the case in the US. Others point to the actual construction of part-time jobs in Britain in a gendered way (Beechey and Perkins, 1987) and until 1994 employers were able to avoid many of the obligations placed upon them by employment legislation if they employed staff for less than 16 hours a week. Part-time work is, of course, only one of a number of working practices, including homeworking, which have collectively come to be called 'flexible' and which employers increasingly turned to in the 1980s. Anna Pollert (1988) has quite rightly pointed out that there is nothing particularly 'new' about employers searching for ways to maximize the exploitation of labour: what perhaps is different is the extent to which employers were aided in their strategy during the 1980s in Britain by government policy.

Occupational segregation by sex has historically been a feature of British labour markets and has remained surprisingly resilient throughout the twentieth century. Not only do most men and women do different jobs in different kinds of industries but a sexual hierarchy also exists where men's jobs are predominantly ranked higher than those carried out by women. Nevertheless, there are now some long-term trends which point to an improvement in the numbers of white women, at least, working in higher-grade jobs. According to longitudinal data collected by the Department of Employment, while there has been a significant increase in the occupational category defined as corporate managers and administrators over the past decade, the growth has been most marked among women. The expansion in employment opportunities in this category was paralleled by increased earnings.

Nevertheless, all recent analyses of women in the labour market indicate that ethnic minority women are not sharing in these gains. Quite the reverse, not only are they over-represented in areas of occupational decline and under-represented in the growth sectors, but they are also likely to be working longer hours, in poorer conditions for lower pay than white women. Ethnic minority women are also at least twice as likely to be unemployed than white women (Roberts, 1994).

Elsewhere in the occupational structure there is evidence to suggest that clerical occupations are slipping down the relative earnings hierarchy and part-time jobs as a whole appear to have a major negative effect upon earnings growth (Elias and Gregory, 1992). In addition, there has been a steady decline in women's employment in operative, assembly and secretarial work. These apparent 'winners' and 'losers' need to be set against a backcloth of a long-term decline in full-time male employment and a labour market where racialized segregation and exclusion are deeply etched. Our sense is that changes in the external labour market are to a large extent reflected closely in the homeworking labour force.

Of all the processes listed above, the most important influencing the incidence of homework is the extent to which enterprises are increasing labour flexibility. Most homeworkers are a prime example of what is often referred to as a 'contingent' workforce as their labour can be treated as a completely variable factor. Homeworking provides an opportunity to reduce labour costs, benefits and other overheads. As we shall in Chapter 5, even in a situation where firms provide identical contracts and conditions for their in-house workers and their homeworkers, considerable benefits accrue from their homeworking labour force in terms of increased productivity and savings on accommodation.

The polarization in skill is also reflected in the diversity of the homeworking labour force, which includes professional occupations as well as clerical and manual work. In much of this book we will be documenting the diversity of homework in Britain. There are few jobs being carried out in the external labour market that are not also being carried out at home. But it should be noted at the outset that the increase in the proportion of women going out to work also affects demand for low-cost (and therefore low-paid), home-based child-minding.

Ethnic variation in women's work is also reflected in the home-based labour force with minority group women over-represented in manufacturing homework in the US, Canada and throughout Europe (Chapkis and Enloe, 1983; Morokvasic et al., 1986; Wakewich, 1989). As we shall see in Chapter 3, all of the ethnic differences in women's employment apparent in the external labour market are mirrored in the home.

WORK IDENTITIES

Whereas in the 1960s and early 1970s debates on gender and employment concentrated on explaining women's entry into the labour force in the post-war period, debate in the 1980s concentrated on the nature of women's employment and changes in it, as discussed above. This debate focused overwhelmingly on the structural basis of occupational segregation by sex and paid less attention to how women workers themselves saw their roles and responsibilities. More recently, the literature has taken more account of these perceptions but in rather different ways.

In Britain, two distinct arguments are currently dominating the debate. On the one hand is the work of Rosemary Crompton and Kay Sanderson (1990) who provide evidence to show that women increasingly recognize the need to seek and retain full-time employment careers (in order to maintain earnings). This recognition has, they argue, increased pressure on employers to offer a range of 'flexible' working practices and is reflected in women's determination to hold on to their jobs when their children are born. Similarly, Hewitt (1993) shows how expectations about working time need to be altered so that the timing of employment throughout the day, week and lifetime allows for fluctuations in men's and women's family obligations.

But there is another perspective which stresses differences between women and men in work aspirations and career development and which argues that women are satisfied with adverse terms and conditions because their primary commitment is to the domestic sphere. Catherine Hakim (1991) has explored the role of women's perceptions about work in an article entitled 'Grateful slaves and self-made women: fact and fantasy in women's work orientations'. The article is theoretically sympathetic to what has been termed the 'new home economics', which regards the traditional sexual division of labour where men are breadwinners and women stay at home as an outcome of rational decision-making in family units. We will quote at some length from this article so that the reader gets a feel of the Hakim argument and our response to it.

Hakim argues that 'although job segregation concentrates women in the lowest status and lowest paid jobs in the workforce, women are disproportionately satisfied with their jobs' (Hakim, 1991: 101). She assesses attitudinal data on the strength of women's work commitment in Western industrial societies and concludes that it is markedly lower than men's work commitment. Work commitment, she argues, is a powerful predictor of women's work decisions and job choices. 'The majority of women aim for a homemaker career in which paid work is of secondary or peripheral importance with strong support from their husbands for this strategy' (Hakim, 1991: 101). Hakim goes on to argue that 'The paradox of women's disproportionate and apparently non-rational satisfaction with the worst jobs is highlighted in the extreme case of homework, which is found in virtually all countries and is almost universally done by women only' (1991: 103). Higher than average levels of job satisfaction among homeworkers are explained as follows:

> Their daily journey to work is reduced to nothing, and their part-time work hours can be fitted in flexibly to the most convenient times of the day or week. When asked why they are doing homework the majority of men and women enumerate all the advantages, emphasising particularly the sense of freedom and flexibility it offers, rather than simply saying they could not find any thing better. (Hakim, 1991: 109)

The argument here is that homeworkers value 'the convenience factors over the high pay and security of employment conventionally valued by men' (1991: 113). Women who do choose to pursue full-time careers have, Hakim argues, higher levels of work commitment. Thus Hakim concludes that theory and research on women's employment seems particularly prone to an over-socialised view of women or with structural factors so heavily weighted that choice flies out of the window . . . in Western industrialised societies at least women's lives are becoming self-made almost as much as men's lives . . . they have a large measure of freedom in the choice of occupation and of husband. Yet most still choose occupations and husbands which maintain traditional views of women's roles. (Hakim, 1991: 114)

Indeed, Hakim argues that the persistence of job segregation should be regarded as a reflection of women's own preferences and choices with a time lag for employers to catch up (1991: 114).

We have a number of reservations about Hakim's analysis. First, the empirical evidence for differences between men's and women's work commitment is much more mixed than Hakim allows, and needs to be seen against the overall increase in women's work commitment among young women for which her own data provide a source. Marsden et al. (1993) show in the case of data on gender disparities in organizational commitment in the United States that difference can be fully accounted for by 'job' rather than 'gender' factors. Marsden et al. (1993) show that organizational commitment is highly correlated with job characteristics which facilitate participation, individual mobility and career development. Men have more and women have less access to the features which enhance commitment. There are also serious problems in using hours of work as an indication or index of work commitment, although this has been a convenient assumption for employers who do not wish to include part-timers in pension schemes or training programmes. A study in Britain by the Institute of Manpower Studies in 1992 found that staff working part-time, flexible hours or job sharing were considered by their employers to be 'more efficient, enthusiastic and committed' than their full-time equivalents (Hewitt, 1993: 116), and the Institute of Personnel Management recognizes that absenteeism and turnover of part-time staff is not markedly higher than for full-timers (Hewitt, 1993).

Secondly, Hakim unquestioningly accepts male evaluations of what constitutes a 'good' job. Not only does she refuse to accept that the situation of women may mean that they apply different criteria in evaluating jobs, she uses women's different criteria as evidence that these women, actively putting forward values of their own, amount to no more than 'grateful slaves', appreciating jobs which men would disdain. Such an understanding of women's work options shows no awareness that the ordinary working day is a 'man-made day' and in no way gender-neutral.

Thirdly, we would like to consider the notion of 'choice' and women's freedom to choose between homemaker and career roles. Hakim argues that authors such as Crompton and Sanderson relegate women to victims of structure so that 'choice flies out of the window'. There are several issues at stake here. First, Crompton and Sanderson (1990) clearly state that their theoretical position is one which takes both structure and action into account and the case studies demonstrate clearly how some women as active protagonists are in a position to make real choices even when confronted by a whole range of external constraints, but most of these women are full-time workers and are better qualified. Women who do not possess these qualifications do not have such 'choices'. If we look, for instance, at the average weekly earnings of women in manufacturing, sales or manual service jobs, we have one simple reason why they have very little 'choice' about having to hitch themselves up with a male wage. Secondly, Hakim puts a good deal of emphasis on full-time work being a proxy measure of work commitment. In Britain today many more ethnic minority women work full-time than white women (70 per cent as against 50 per cent). The vast majority of these ethnic minority women have not 'chosen' to pursue a career over the homemaker role; they work full-time through financial necessity, a necessity which is linked to higher rates of black male unemployment, larger family size, lower household incomes and the necessity of working longer hours to bring home something approximating a living wage (Phizacklea, 1994). As we shall see in Chapter 3, Asian women do not work at home because their husbands want them to, most are working at home because of restricted employment alternatives, high levels of male unemployment and inadequate state benefits.

This raises a final objection to the Hakim view. Social scientists have good reason to be sceptical about the high levels of job satisfaction expressed by all workers in surveys, including those in low-paid work, and that is because if one taps attitudes to job satisfaction in ways other than the standard question one gets very different outcomes. For instance, the 1981 Department of Employment Homeworking Survey indicated that only 5 per cent (rising to 11 per cent in the case of manufacturing homeworkers) claimed to be dissatisfied with their jobs (Hakim, 1987a). Hakim argues for the importance of asking 'meaningful questions' in the measurement of job satisfaction. We believe that the wide-ranging questions that we asked homeworkers in our research are perfectly 'meaningful' (we carefully piloted the schedules) and yet, as we shall see in the pages that follow, the homeworkers are quick to point out that the seeming advantages of working at home contain real disadvantages as well. Hakim's data document different work history trajectories among women, showing that an increasing number of women set off on careers and time their child-bearing, for instance, to fit around the career, whereas for others, finding work which fits round their family roles is the main goal. Our view is that this does not indicate the irrelevance of structural factors but rather that these differing outcomes are the result of a complex interaction between structure and agency as we hope to illustrate in the example of Asian women homeworkers. They could hardly be described as 'grateful slaves'!

THE MEANING OF 'HOME'

Homework needs to be contextualized not only in terms of the wider labour market but also in terms of ideological definitions. We feel it is important not to allow the 'home' in home-based work to become an unproblematic, natural category in the analysis. The appearance of the domestic sphere as a private domain, outside the truly social space of work and politics, is a Victorian middle-class construction; its privatization was founded on the exclusion of women from paid work and their idealization as morally superior 'angels in the house'. Hence it is no wonder that those who work at home have to struggle to make their work visible and recognized as work. This is one reason why, since the 1970s, feminist sociologists have insisted on documenting the amount of labour which women continue to expend in their homes, producing goods and services for members of the household, even when they go out to work (for instance, Berk, 1985; Oakley, 1974). Others have uncovered the violence and sexual exploitation which our notions of amicable and egalitarian family relations obscure from view (Dobash and Dobash, 1992; Pahl, 1985). Nowadays, the home as a place of 'confinement and stultification' rarely appears in discussions of homeworking. Rather, the 'home-working family' is seen as making work a pleasure by reintegrating it with family life. In the mid-1980s President Reagan's campaign to deregulate homework in the United States was promoted in this way. In a new version of the Victorian contrast between home and the harsh outside world, we now humanize work by bringing it into the home. Property columns encourage us to become 'new ruralists' by buying an 'enchanted thatched cottage' to fill with computer equipment (*Independent on Sunday*, 25 April 1993: 68–71). Revived and revised images of domestic life are not confined to images of home-based work, of course: nor are they simply a matter of representation. Privatization in social welfare and housing policy increasingly defines the home as the axis of British social life.

Since the domestic sphere is an ideological category, not simply a physical space, researchers on home-based work need to take into account the material and cultural context in which homeworking respondents construct the meaning of their work, their participation in the labour force and their identities as family members. While clearly we must pay close attention to what informants say, both good and bad, about their work, we should also be asking about the contexts and social locations which encourage an attitude of compromise and acceptance or allow for criticism or resistance. This is not simply a matter of how far women respondents accept conventional gender roles or their location in the domestic sphere, but also a question of their location in class and racialized social hierarchies and the political perspectives these may engender.

If the ideological meaning of the domestic sphere is historically variable, 'homes' are also highly differentiated in material terms. So long as women bear primary responsibility for children and domestic labour, relationships to the home will be gender-specific, but that is not to say they are uniform. In addition to important differences in the conditions governing the paid work which women do at home, as between professional, clerical and manufacturing work, for instance, there are important material differences in women's homes as working environments. Differences in terms of comfort, light and space and the amount and kind of labour which is required on a day-to-day basis to keep both domestic and paid work 'ticking over' vary enormously between households and will make for critical differences between women in the meaning of working at home.

Homeworking thus embodies many of the issues women in the labour market face: the combination of paid and unpaid household responsibilities and the different experiences and material circumstances of homeworking women in an ethnically and class-divided society.

A HETEROGENEOUS WORKFORCE

It is argued, therefore, that an analysis of the position of women homeworkers allows us better to understand not only the gendering process but also the specific constraints that operate on all women workers (and not simply those who work at home), including the need for work that can be fitted around household responsibilities.

To reiterate, the 'home' is not a gender-neutral category but is filled with gendered meanings. It is assumed to be perfectly natural that women stay at home and look after children. The fact that they may also want or have to earn money is regarded as less 'natural': home is not the place of work and therefore homeworkers' jobs are not treated as 'real jobs'. Men are expected to leave the confines of the home and go out to work; when they do work at home it is rarely in order to resolve a child-care problem and they may express the fear that 'the neighbours don't think I've got a real job anymore' (quoted in Huws et al., 1990: 68).

We want to suggest that the constraints imposed by the remarkable persistence of gendered ideologies is something that all women homeworkers share. But the homeworking labour force is heterogeneous; it is cross-cut by ethnicity and class in ways that are often quite subtle and impossible to discern from aggregate national data sets. We have seen already the impossibility of talking about a general category of 'women' in the labour market because racialization has etched such deep and persisting lines into an already sexually segregated labour market. The fact that racial discrimination has been outlawed in Britain for nearly 30 years has not prevented even overt forms of employment discrimination taking place (McCrudden et al., 1991).

But racial discrimination can take more hidden or indirect forms as well. For instance, employers may not advertise jobs externally or only advertise jobs in particular places, where only certain people will get to know about the availability of specific types of employment. In these cases the employer may not be deliberately trying to exclude certain applicants but he or she is still discriminating in an indirect way because not everyone has an equal opportunity to apply for the job. We shall see how many of the Asian women in our home city of Coventry have taken up homeworking because of a complex set of factors involving the circumstances of their husbands, the benefit system and the opportunities available to them. But their jobs as homeworkers are even further constrained because their friendship networks are more likely to bring them into contact with work in the badly paid clothing industry than in some of the better remunerated forms of homeworking in the city. Many black and ethnic minority women live in households where the collective income is well below average, but so do many white women homeworkers.

The question of social class is also ethnic and gender laden. As we have seen many more women are entering managerial positions now than was the case ten years ago, but it is still low when compared to men. Research carried out in the early 1980s indicated that only 8 per cent of women with fathers in professional or managerial positions obtained jobs comparable to those of their father (Heath, 1981). We know that a good deal of sex discrimination in employment has been rationalized on the grounds that 'women are not really interested in a career, they'll just leave to start a family'. Of course, there is some truth in this; as Britain has the worst *per capita* preschool child-care provision in Europe, many women have no choice but to give up their jobs when they have a child. Many women who take up homeworking believe that this is the way that they can maintain their career and still 'be a good mother'. Unfortunately, what we find is that the demands of work and children are often irreconcilable. But many of those women who see homeworking as a way of continuing their career without a break are already well qualified and well paid and are not only able to translate those advantages into a home-based job, but can also afford to send their children to a child-minder for at least part of their working day. Some of the women who talk about their work in this book have a university degree and professional qualifications as well. Some, in addition, are living with a partner who has similar qualifications and scarce skills which are rewarded highly in the formal labour market. Their combined earnings lift their average household income well above the average. But we did not uncover any ethnic minority households in this position.

We are not saying that the more 'privileged' home-working women do not experience the pressures, isolation and many of the other disadvantages of working at home, but they do not share in the real material hardship experienced by so many other homeworkers. What we are saying therefore is that we need to take into account the heterogeneity of the homeworking labour force and the opportunities and constraints that different positions in ethnic and class relations bring to an already sexually segregated labour market.

The question of the meaning of home-based work will not be resolved simply through the provision of more data. Long-standing, contrasting images of homework were amply documented nearly ten years ago, yet they maintain their currency despite nearly ten years of research on and innovation in home-based work. While we therefore do not expect more information to resolve the issues (there are too many interests at stake), we hope that the data we provide will lead to a more informed discussion of recent trends and a recognition of the great diversity within the homeworking labour force.

2   Finding out about Homeworking

Our aim in this book is to bring together what is already known about homeworking with new information that we have gathered ourselves. All research has its strengths and weaknesses, and in this chapter we look critically at some of the research that has been carried out on homeworking in Britain and other advanced industrial countries. We go on to explain why and how we carried out our own research on homeworking.

We want to argue that some of the seeming polarity in the debate around home-based work can be explained by differing methodologies and sampling procedures. For instance, the evidence collected by local homeworking research projects, officers and campaigns on the incidence and persistence of extremely low-paid, arduous, manu-facturing home-based work in the UK has often only been possible after the building of trust between project workers and home-based workers. These surveys and projects have documented extremely low wages earned in a variety of manufacturing industries, especially but not only clothing fashionwear, and have found that in some parts of the country the number of manufacturing homeworkers is increasing rather than shrinking. But because these surveys have been conducted largely in the inner cities they have had little to say about non-manual home-workers and whether the latter face particular problems.

At the other extreme, hardly a day goes by without a

press story or news clip on the advantages of 'tele-working'. This much more 'glamorous' image of homeworking was given some empirical support by the Department of Employment programme of research which also emphasized the increasing importance of non-manual home-based work and associated this with high rates of worker satisfaction (Hakim, 1984, 1987a, b). The pro-gramme was explicitly designed to demonstrate the diversity of conditions and earnings in home-based work and to dispel the image of the home worker as tied down by family demands and forced to work for low wages. Home-based workers were widely defined and included all those working at home, including the self-employed, freelance workers and labour only contractors. Excluding child-minders, it was estimated that in 1981 there were 229,800 homeworkers in Britain. It argued that although manufacturing home-based work still accounted for nearly a third of those working at home, it was becoming a 'relative rarity' when compared with the much larger number of those working at home in a wide range of occupations. It also argued that ethnic minorities were under-represented in the home-based workforce (Hakim, 1987a). In fact, in the later fuller report of the research, Hakim (1987b) admitted that the 1981 National Home-working Survey did not provide any information on the proportion of all homeworkers who belong to ethnic minorities.

The picture drawn by the Department of Employment (DE) was one of workers who had the ability to exercise choice over their employment options and who were working at home because of its positive advantages. The DE programme of research did not help the cause of organizations which had campaigned for years to raise public awareness of the constraints which force many thousands of women into homeworking and which have sought to achieve concrete improvements through legislative change (for example, employee status for all homeworkers). Indeed, evidence produced by the DE survey (which we will later critique) has frequently been used by the British government to argue that further regulation of home-based work is unnecessary. In the words of one Conservative MP: 'As the survey shows, working at home is the result of choice because one of the often-quoted advantages of homeworking is the sense of freedom and independence that it gives' (Mr Baptiste MP, Elmet, Conservative: *Hansard*, 17 May, 1989: 398). And as the then Minister for Employment described the situation, homeworking 'is ticking over nicely'.

Given the countervailing though fragmented evidence from local homeworking officers and groups, our concern was to carry out research which provided an up-to-date picture of home-based work as we entered the 1990s, avoiding what we identified as the sampling problems of the DE research. One of the key issues we faced was definitional. For instance, some people who work at home are supplied with work from one source only while others have a number of suppliers. Other people who work at home produce and sell goods and services 'on their own account'. Many studies have in the past differentiated between 'homeworkers', who are subordinated to the supplier of the work and who do not trade on their own account, and other home-based workers. However, in our study, we wished to explore similarities and differences across the whole range of home-based work and we therefore use the term 'homeworker' to describe all our respondents whether they describe themselves as employees, self-employed or 'running my own business' or whether they are referred to as 'homeworkers' or 'teleworkers'.

We are well aware that putting manual and non-manual work together defies conventional categories and assumptions about what are regarded as key determinants of occupational status, rewards and job satisfaction. Nevertheless, we use the term 'homeworker' because one of our key arguments in this book is that relationships to the home and in the home are highly gender specific. Using the broad category of homeworker highlights the gendered aspects of women's home-based work, even though the character of that work will also reflect the impact of class and racialization. Prugl (1990) has gone as far as to suggest that there is a need for a feminist definition which stresses the location of the work in the home rather than simply making reference to the relationship to the supplier or the fact that the work is located remotely. As we shall see, even among the highly rewarded and what could be considered to be privileged ranks of information and communication technology (ICT) homeworkers, both the reasons for working at home and the experience of homeworking are quite different for women compared with men.

Before turning to recent research evidence we want to consider briefly some of the historical evidence on the incidence of homeworking. What we know about home-working historically comes largely from documents recording debates about how to regulate or eliminate it. Some of these debates were between middle-class social reformers; some were between these reformers and men and women in the labour movement. Homework has always straddled a range of interests concerning appropriate work and family roles for men and women, as well as the differing interests of employers, reformers, other waged workers and homeworkers themselves.

THE HISTORICAL RECORD: PROPER WORK FOR WOMEN?

We have suggested that the view that a woman's rightful place is in the home, caring for her husband and children, is a Victorian middle-class construction. But such a view has given rise to very different evaluations of the place of homework in women's lives. Daniels (1989) provides evidence to suggest that social reformers in the United States at the turn of the century were keen to eliminate homeworking because they regarded it as undermining men's role as breadwinners and women's roles as mothers and carers. They were keen to uphold the separation of home and work (see also Boris, 1989). In contrast, Pennington and Westover (1989) argue that in Victorian times homeworking was considered to be one of the few respectable forms of work for married women in Britain because it did *not* conflict with the view that a woman's rightful place was in the home. In their historical account of homeworking, they quote from a late nineteenth-century novel, *Mrs Haliburton's Troubles*:

> The evils of women going out to work in the factories have been rehearsed over and over again; and the chief evil – we will put all others out of sight – is, that it takes the married woman from her home and family. But with glove making the case is different. While the husbands are abroad at the manufactories pursuing their daily work, the wives and elder daughters are earning money easily and pleasantly at home. (quoted in Pennington and Westover, 1989: 15)

The Industrial Revolution constituted an important ideological break in conceptions of home and work, particularly in what constituted an appropriate sexual division of labour. Nevertheless, it did not constitute a complete productive break between home and factory. Not only was that division very uneven depending upon the industry and the region, but in many cases the Industrial Revolution initiated a more complex division of labour in production which allowed for the fragmentation of previously skilled tasks. One of the best examples is the clothing industry. In 1846 the introduction of the sewing machine went a long way to revolutionizing production methods, allowing for the fragmentation of tasks and the substitution of unskilled for skilled labour. Whereas this facilitated the move from home to factory in some parts of Britain, the historian Sally Alexander argues that in London it simply transformed the productiveness of women homeworkers (Alexander, 1983: 48). While the high costs of fuel and rent in London were important factors, it was the abundance of cheap female and immigrant labour trapped in London's docklands that largely accounted for these disparities. In other industries, such as boot and shoe manufacturing, some processes were mechanized while others were left to hand craft in the home. In particular, homeworkers have always provided a cheap and flexible workforce in industries where short, unstandardized production remains a key feature.

The survival of homeworking throughout the process of industrialization and beyond has in no way been unique to Britain; evidence from France (Morokvasic et al., 1986) and the United States (Boris, 1989; Daniels, 1989; Silver, 1989) indicates the same pattern of development and survival. While Britain and France were countries of immigration in the late nineteenth century, the scale of those migrations is totally dwarfed by the scale of migration and settlement at that time in the United States. The historical literature on homeworking in the US indicates a heavy reliance on immigrant labour from the late nineteenth century through to the 1940s by which time homework had become regulated or outlawed on a national scale by the Fair Labor Standards Act (Dangler, 1989). As in Britain and France, the US clothing industry was heavily reliant upon homeworkers. Nevertheless, one account of homeworking in New York at the turn of the century indicates that making artificial flowers and feathers, sorting coffee beans, wig-making and cigar-rolling were some of the hundred occupations undertaken by an estimated 250,000 homeworkers in the city in 1910 (Daniels, 1989: 15).

But there is little doubt that after this date *officially* estimated numbers of homeworkers in both Britain and the US (and to a certain extent in France as well) began to decline. If mechanization and homeworking had by the early twentieth century found a 'happy' accommodation, why was this the case? We would want to argue that the apparent answers to that question may not paint a completely accurate picture because we do not know how much homework was driven underground by subsequent legislation in Britain and the US. Moves to regulate homework came as early as the 1880s in Britain with concern over the sweated conditions that home-workers laboured under coming from both social reformers and trade unions. By 1888 the Select Committee on the Sweating System had been set up in Britain and gave official backing to this concern. In 1901 the Factory and Workshop Act was passed which required employers to keep lists of homeworkers so that in theory inspectors could visit the homes of these workers (Pennington and Westover, 1989). This was not a particularly satisfactory form of regulation as it was argued that 'The giver out of work must be compelled under very stringent conditions and with very heavy penalties attached to keep an absolutely complete list of his workers. He does not do it now, he has never done it, and he will never do it under existing law' (Report of the National Conference on Sweated Industries quoted in Roxby, 1984: 136). Few prosecutions were brought under the Act.

Another way in which attempts were made to regulate homeworking was by setting down a national minimum wage in the lowest paid industries. In 1907 a select parliamentary committee recommended the establishment of Trade Boards to set minimum rates of pay (Phizacklea, 1990). In 1909 the Trade Boards Act was passed setting minimum wages in men's tailoring, cardboard box making, chain making and machine-made lace making. Pennington and Westover argue that the Trade Boards did make a difference in improving the wages of some homeworkers, while at the same time reducing one of the main incentives for employers to use homeworkers – the cheapness of their labour (Pennington and Westover, 1989: 110). Nevertheless, they also argue that it was extremely easy for employers to evade the legislation and that homeworkers themselves colluded in that evasion because they needed the work. Detailed research on the use of homeworkers in the clothing industry has come to similar conclusions (Phizacklea, 1990: 30).

Some trade unionists in Britain were keen to organize homeworkers and spent much time and energy doing so, while others in the movement wanted homeworking abolished altogether as it was regarded as undermining indoor labour, a view which was wholly endorsed by organized labour on the other side of the Atlantic. By 1874 the Cigar Makers International Union in the US were campaigning against homeworkng on the grounds of its health risks and use of child labour (Daniels, 1989: 20). While the campaign led to legislation prohibiting home-work in New York State, manufacturers successfully challenged the law as exceeding police powers. As a result, Daniels argues that the presence or absence of homework in a particular industry largely reflected the level of organization and militancy of its unionized workers (1989: 20). By 1919 the combined efforts of reformers and trade unionists had secured legislation which either regulated or prohibited homework in 13 states (Porter Benson, 1989: 54). In 1933 homework became federally regulated under the National Recovery Administration which banned homework in over a hundred industries, and while this legislation was also declared unconstitutional the spirit of the law was enshrined in the Fair Labor Standards Act of 1938.

The politics of Reaganite deregulation led to a concerted move to contest and overturn this US legislation from the mid-1980s onwards. The arguments for change harked back to Victorian constructions of home life. For instance, in 1985 Representative Newt Gingrich from Georgia reintroduced the Family Opportunity Act into the US Congress; its purpose, he argued, was 'to restore the family setting by allowing families to learn and earn together at home' (Christensen, 1985: 9). At the same time Senator Hatch of Utah introduced the Freedom of the Workplace Act which he argued would provide the 'opportunity for women, particularly those with small children, to work at home without all the encumbrances of the Fair Labor Standards Act restrictions' (Christensen, 1985: 10). In Britain, the same politics of de-regulation led to the abolition of the Wages Councils in 1993 (which succeeded the Trade Boards), removing the last safeguard on minimum wages for some of the most vulnerable homeworkers. It is within this context that we consider some of the contemporary evidence on homeworking.

CONTEMPORARY TRENDS

In what follows we look at some of the larger studies that have been carried out in Britain and the United States, considering the strengths and weaknesses of each study and, where appropriate, how it helped us to conduct our own research.

In Britain, two large-scale studies of home-based working were conducted in 1979–80 and 1981 respectively. The West Yorkshire Homeworking Survey carried out between 1979 and 1980 was based on a door-to-door survey of 4,000 households producing 90 interviews with home-based workers (Allen and Wolkowitz, 1987a). It found manufacturing home-based work to be more extensive than the DE survey which followed a year later, with earnings much lower than average despite long hours of work, and typified by the absence of much real flexibility in combining waged and unwaged work in the home. The survey was conducted in working-class neighbourhoods and therefore was unable (and did not intend) to provide much data on white-collar homework.

Sheila Allen and Carol Wolkowitz introduced many themes which have become central to the analysis of homework in Britain. In particular, they analysed home-work as a method of production in which profits were based on the casualization of labour, and saw it as evidence of the adverse impact that deregulation would have for workers' security of employment as well as earnings. Secondly, they identified various mechanisms through which suppliers control work done in workers' homes which, along with domestic timetables, constrain the actual autonomy of people doing paid work in their own homes.

Gender was central to the analysis in a number of ways. First, the research highlighted the ways in which the gendered character of models of employment in advanced industrial societies renders paid and unpaid work at home invisible. Allen and Wolkowitz argue that the pre-dominant model of employment assumes the separation of home and work. It is a model of work that adopts the able-bodied adult male working pattern as the norm and which therefore produces a distorted picture of who 'workers' are, where they work and what are typical working hours and routines. The pervasiveness and persistence of this model means that homeworkers', as well as many other women's, work that does not fit this model is discounted, treated as occurring under exceptional circumstances or simply marginal to the mainstream labour force.

In other words, the construction of homework in the light of dominant ideological parameters surrounding definitions of the labour force and both the spatial and temporal location of work is central to the Allen and Wolkowitz analysis. Their analysis draws attention to the contradiction between the ways in which homework is represented according to dominant ideology, such as 'pin money', 'turning a hobby into an additional source of household income', 'increased autonomy' and so on and the reality of homework for many of their respondents: long hours, punctuated by strict deadlines from employers, demanding family members and a reliance on homework for a regular household income.

Secondly, Allen and Wolkowitz see the sexual division of labour, especially women's responsibility for unpaid work, as the key factor producing a homeworking labour force. They emphasize the role of both the constraints facing mothers of young children and aged carers of elderly relatives and the id constraints affecting women more generally. Racisi labour market and discrimination against the disabled were seen as important additional factors. As was typical of feminist writing of the time, however, the analysis focused primarily on commonalities in the experience of women and the data on the wages and conditions of work of the ten Asian homeworkers in the sample were not analysed separately. One of the main arguments was that homeworking was fully integrated into the main body of industrial production and employment in Britain and the authors were wary of providing any fuel for the kind of press reporting of ethnic minority homework which exoticized homework, in order to marginalize its role in the economy or negate its importance in the work histories of a broad cross-section of British women. In retrospect, it appears that while these points are still valid, attention to the differences in the situations of white and ethnic minority women and what these mean for developing an adequate political strategy on homework is now a greater priority.

In the event, however, it was a different focus on gender which was picked up and used in a way which Allen and Wolkowitz certainly had not intended. Chapter 5 of *Homeworking: Myths and Realities* (Allen and Wolkowitz, 1987a), was concerned to introduce a recognition of the power relations within which homeworkers organize their paid and unpaid work. This involved paying attention to supplier deadlines but also, it was argued, the expectations of family members, including especially husbands. They also provided evidence that a small proportion of the informants seemed to collude with the husband in defining homework as non-work, so propping up his status as breadwinner. Catherine Hakim has since picked up on this discussion, using it in her argument, that we have already critiqued in Chapter 1, that some women gratefully accept slave status, willingly servicing their husbands' whims rather than developing careers of their own. Hakim argues that women who willingly marry and accept the authority of such husbands should take the blame for their poor situation in the labour market rather than seek explanations in structural factors.

This seems to us an unwarranted use of the data presented in *Homeworking: Myths and Realities*, unless one could show that the structural constraints the women were rationalizing no longer exist. Moreover, in what follows we will provide ample evidence of the extent to which homeworkers resent their husbands and families trivializing their home-based work. More importantly, however, is that a division in the female labour force between those women who put their families first, and those who develop lifetime careers is now quite central to the organization of production and reproduction in Western societies and simply cannot be seen as the result of women's own choices; the work of reproducing labour still has to be done and no one can point to an influx of men into this kind of work. Although it may be true that no one forces women to do this kind of work in the way that the concept of 'patriarchy' perhaps implies (though one would have to raise the question of the role of violent husbands), women will continue to do it for their families not only because they have internalized these responsibilities but because there is no alternative given the persistence of segregated low-paid work and the high price of child-care and domestic services.

We still think it is correct to pay particular attention to the ideological construction of women's work, including homework. While it is true to say that many homeworkers work at home because of the absence of adequate child-care, or because they prefer to look after their children themselves, it is also the case that ideological expectations about women's work roles continue to rationalize what now appear to be deteriorating conditions for many working women. An increasing proportion of work opportunities, especially among new jobs, are part-time, casualized jobs in the service sector offering few career opportunities. There is an investment in this kind of work opportunity which goes way beyond women's own choices. More to the point, it is not clear why, as Hakim implies, only those willing or able to undertake full-time, male-pattern career jobs are entitled to employment rights or career status.

A year after the Allen and Wolkowitz study, the Department of Employment survey of home-based work was carried out based on 576 interviews. The spring 1981 Labour Force Survey (LFS) was used as the sift survey and sampling frame for a specially designed interview survey of home-based workers which was carried out by the Office of Population Censuses and Surveys (OPCS) in the autumn of 1981. While it is regarded as the most authoritative source of information on home-based work, we would suggest that, apart from now being out of date, there are also problems of interpretation and sampling. The data are restricted to England and Wales only and no data are given on the tasks undertaken by homeworkers, their systems of payment or their suppliers.

In addition, because of sampling and response rate problems we believe that the true extent of manufacturing homeworking, particularly among ethnic minorities, is probably underestimated by the survey for the following reasons. The LFS is based on a random sample but manufacturing home-based work is not randomly distributed but highly concentrated in areas such as inner London, a traditional centre of clothing manufacturing home-based work. But the response rate in London was only 43 per cent and no information is given about the response rate in other cities. While Hakim (1987b) admits that language represents one particular barrier to working in factories and offices, there is no indication in the report that language might in itself have been a significant factor in reducing the response rate in cities where ethnic minorities are residentially concentrated. Our own extensive experience of working with ethnic minority women (see, for instance, Phizacklea, 1990) indicates that unless mother tongue interviewers are used in certain localities there is no possibility of interviewing homeworkers.

Another factor concerns disillusionment with research; in 1992 we sought the employment aspirations of Bangladeshi women homeworkers in Tower Hamlets. The homeworkers complained that surveys of employment aspirations in their community had never led to any material improvement in their situation. The homeworkers concerned were unwilling to participate in any further research unless they could be convinced that there was a real prospect that surveys would lead to concrete measures to deal with the problems they themselves identified (Mitter et al., 1993). In addition, fear of racial attack can act as a deterrent to answering the door to a stranger and because so much home-based work is 'off the books' many home-based workers are reluctant to declare themselves. The experience of local homeworking projects is that it is only after many years of building trust between the project workers and home-based workers that the latter feel able to talk openly about their work (see, for instance, the report of the Wolverhampton Homeworkers Research Project, 1984).

There is often a refusal to recognize the difficulty of surveying home-based workers through conventional methods by those who compile labour market data, and a refusal to accept the results of non-random surveys, despite the fact that these are the only ones in which many home-based workers will participate. Moreover, the idea that people will participate in a survey only if some personal improvement is offered offends the scientific sensibilities of many researchers and funders seeking objective, unbiased data. At the other extreme, feminist methodology, which has seen itself based explictly on the standpoint of women has emphasized the inadequacies of the 'survey method' for studying women, partly on the grounds that survey questionnaires provide a set format, that they oversimplify by forcing choices and ask the wrong questions (Harding, 1987; Maguire, 1987; Smith, 1987). Rather, feminist methodology has privileged ethnographic over survey methods, the emphasis here being on empowering participatory research methods.

In this respect the National Group on Homeworking's national survey of homeworkers (1994), while not defined as 'feminist research', also represents an important innovation in research methodology. The National Group, founded in 1984, is an organization of homeworkers, local government officers, regional low pay units, trade unionists and academics campaigning in homeworkers' interests. It recognized that although some of its members had been involved in or undertaken local surveys the Group lacked national data to back up its assertions about the extent of manufacturing homeworking and homeworkers' low wages and lack of employment rights. Thus the Group decided to mount its own survey conducting as many interviews as possible across England. The local groups undertook training together and data were collected using the same agreed questionnaire, in order to provide information on the different regions but also make possible comparisons between regions.

This innovative plan proved more difficult to implement than anticipated. Liaison between local officers was time-consuming and, as each had different immediate priorities for data collection, it was difficult to agree which questions should take precedence, many of the questions were not answered by all the interviewees and a third of the sample was not currently working at the time of interview. All the homeworkers were already known to the local campaigns and officers and, apart from the obvious biases this could introduce, there was the additional problem that some campaigns, for instance in Birmingham, had targeted a particular group: for example, Asian women in the clothing industry. However, because the sample was made up of homeworkers who either made contact with a local campaign or who were contacted by a campaign, it successfully captured the situation of the least satisfied and most exploited homeworkers. For instance, there is only one clerical homeworker in the sample of 175 homeworkers and no information and communication technology homeworkers at all. The aim of the National Group has always been to raise awareness and to campaign for an improvement in the situation of the most vulnerable groups of homeworkers and this is reflected in the survey.

The sample of 175 included 90 white, 6 black, 64 Asian, 8 'other' and 7 missing cases (11 were men) in Leeds, Rochdale, London, Nottingham, Birmingham, Manchester, Leicester, Wakefield and Calderdale. Some of the main findings of the National Group Survey are as follows. Of those homeworkers who answered the multiple-choice question on why they did homework, 'money' and 'child-care' were mentioned by over 90 per cent. All but two of the Asian women did sewing at home (to reiterate, this may reflect various campaigns' focus on the clothing industry, as in a much smaller sample in Coventry we found Asian women involved in other industries). A third of the sample did not know who their employer was; the median number of hours worked was 32.5 a week; and 83 per cent earned less than £2.50 an hour (National Group on Homeworking, 1994).

The methodological point that we want to make here is that, despite the biases and missing cases that we know to exist in research of this kind, we believe that the prospect of going in 'cold' to explore many areas of homeworking will prove disappointing. The vulnerable situation of the most disadvantaged homeworkers is such that 'official' surveys or random sampling by unknown researchers will find it difficult to contact homeworkers or obtain their cooperation and even the more advantaged may not accept the right of outsiders to information about their private activities.

WHITE-COLLAR HOMEWORKING AND THE
RISE OF THE 'TELEWORKER'

Futurologists have been telling us since 1973 that the era of the 'electronic cottage' is just around the corner (see Bell, 1973). Recently, the media have swamped us with stories about the *arrival* of 'teleworking', how *very* soon we will all be sitting at home doing all the things we used to do in the office with computer conferences and electronic mail to speed things up. This media preoccupation is in fact directed at largely professional jobs, the boring 'paid for the time you are logged on' data entry clerk is not usually featured in these stories, nor the women preparing your Council Tax bill. The growing range of jobs of the latter type are not glamorous enough to make good stories nor so obviously in the 'slave labour' league to warrant media attention. In fact, what most empirical studies of information and communication technology (ICT) homeworking agree upon is how slow the shift from office to home has actually been, with conservative management attitudes a major factor (Olson, 1989).

Having carried out a small and pioneering study of women programmers working at home in the early 1980s, Ursula Huws embarked on a far more ambitious programme of research in the mid- to late-1980s in Britain, France, Germany and Italy. The *Empirica* study as it is known claims to be the most systematic study of ITC homeworking to date and elicited the views of 4,000 managers, 2,500 members of the general public and case studied 14 companies in the four countries. The 'teleworking' sample in these companies is 72 per cent female with three-quarters of these workers having children (Huws et al., 1990: 59). Huws et al. argue against a technologically determinist model of the future of 'teleworking'. Their research indicates that 'teleworking' schemes are only adopted by those managers who see it as solving an immediate, concrete problem such as the retention of valued staff or of cutting costs. In turn, they argue that individuals who become 'teleworkers' do so for equally practical, immediate reasons such as having no alternative or for reasons of child-care; 'the technology is merely a tool. Its role is simply to facilitate the implementation of decisions which have been made for essentially non-technical reasons' (Huws et al., 1990: 219).

In contrast to Huws et al.'s predominantly female sample of ICT homeworkers, Margrethe Olson's (1989) research in the US is based on a largely male sample of 807 'teleworkers' drawn from the subscribers to two trade magazines, one for computer professionals and the other on computing for general professionals. Keeping in mind that we have here two quite separate pieces of research (even carried out in different continents), there are interesting gender differences apparent in the motivation to take up homeworking. In the Huws et al. study, the need felt by women to combine work and child-care was a primary motivating factor for taking up homeworking. Olson's predominantly male sample gave as their primary motivation work-related reasons (Olson, 1989). Over 50 per cent said that the reason they first decided to work at home was 'to increase my productivity', while only 8 per cent responded 'to take care of my family' (Olson, 1989: 224). Enhanced productivity was rated as the biggest advantage of working at home, while over-working was deemed to be a major hazard.

Very few studies of homeworking have looked at both men and women, nor has previous research interviewed both partners in nuclear family structures where at least one person is a homeworker. Thus the research carried out by Leslie Haddon and Roger Silverstone (1993) in the UK marks an interesting departure. While their sample is small, 19 households in which two partners lived together with children, it affords interesting lines of enquiry. In the words of the researchers, 'It is commonly noted that the most challenging environment for the pursuit of telework would be one which contained children, and hence a focus on the nuclear family would provide maximum access to the full range of complicating factors in the teleworking experience' (Haddon and Silverstone, 1993: 5). The in-depth interviews carried out in the study provide confirming evidence of the significant gender differences in motivation and experience of ITC homeworkers revealed in the predominantly single-sex samples of Huws et al. and Olson. In Chapter 5 we build on the accumulated evidence of these studies in considering whether or not ITC homeworking really does offer a better-rewarded and more congenial form of homework for women today. Rather than replicate any of these studies, we concentrated our efforts on a small number of firms and organizations with ITC homeworking schemes and examined what the employers saw as the advantages for themselves and their employees.

Far less research has been carried out on what are more routinized forms of white-collar homeworking. In this respect we found the pioneering work carried out by Kathleen Christensen in the US between 1984 and 1985 both informative and inspiring in so far as it provided us with a methodological model for part of our own research. Christensen (1988a) published a questionnaire in *Family Circle* magazine which is read by 19 million women in the United States. A total of 7,000 women responded, most of whom were clerical workers (including typing, book-keeping, insurance claims rating and data entry work on computers); craftworkers (such as sewing and knitting) and professional occupations (such as accounting, architecture, planning and writing). The Christensen data directly challenge the notion that computers are the central factor in the proliferation of homework: only one in four clerical workers and one in three professionals were using them in their home-based work in 1984. Christensen (1989: 186) argues that 'values related to family, work and money – not technology – drive the initial decision to work at home'.

Christensen found that a large number of the clerical homeworkers in the sample had the legal status of 'independent contractor'. Nevertheless, they worked for only one employer and had little control over the amount and timing of their work. In some cases the women had previously worked in the offices of the same company but the shift to home-based working meant the loss of employee status and the rights and benefits that this brings.

Christensen's research also highlights the flaws in the assumption that homework can reconcile the tension between the need to earn money and the need or desire to care for young children. The vast majority of women in the survey simply did not manage to work when their children were around or awake. Some paid for child-care, others relied on other family members to look after them, while others waited until they were asleep before attempting work. Most homeworking mothers found combining work and child-care stressful and isolating (Christensen, 1985, 1989).

While Christensen's research represents some of the most extensive evidence that we have on homeworking, the *Family Circle*-based research has certain methodological drawbacks:

1 The sample is restricted to the readership of the chosen magazine and this may target certain groups with particular interests, for instance, free patterns will be of particular interest to home dress-makers.
2 Even if the readership were representative of the population as a whole, there may still be class differences in response rate (even with a postage-paid questionnaire).
3 If the magazine is published in English it is inaccessible to non-English speakers.
4 One has no idea how many homeworkers see the questionnaire and fail to fill it in.
5 It is possible that disgruntled home-based workers are more likely to fill it in than those who are satisfied.

Nevertheless, we felt that compared to other methods the Christensen approach had much to recommend it for our own research needs to which we now turn.

OUR OWN RESEARCH METHODS

We decided that if we wanted a reasonable national picture of homeworking, which would both capture those homeworkers who may have previously slipped through the net and be cheap to implement, we would have to use a combination of methods. We decided that putting a questionnaire in a large circulation, national women's magazine would provide us with a national sample at minimum cost. Nevertheless, as the magazine would be published in English, we decided that a smaller in-depth study would also be necessary to explore whether or not ethnic variations in homeworking existed. Finally, we decided to examine in some depth ICT homeworking schemes by taking case study firms and organizations in both the private and public sectors.

The magazine which ran the questionnaire for us is called *Prima*. It is Britain's best-selling women's monthly magazine; the publishers claim a readership of 2,283,000 for the period covering May 1990 when the questionnaire appeared in the magazine. Table 2.1 shows the breakdown in terms of annual household income of our *Prima* readers home-based sample and compares this with all *Prima* readers and a breakdown of all women in the United Kingdom by annual household income. Our *Prima* sample is better represented in the higher socioeconomic bands than *Prima* readers generally who in turn are over-represented in the higher bands and under-represented in the lower bands of household income when compared to the population as a whole. As well as having a sampling frame biased towards the 'better-off', *Prima*'s presumably English-speaking readership will exclude many ethnic minority women. Thus a different method was used for targeting ethnic minority and other home-based workers in city areas.

A total of 403 home-based workers returned questionnaires, many with accompanying letters which afforded a rich source of additional data. (The questionnaire is

Table 2.1   *Annual household income of* Prima *homeworkers compared to* Prima *readership and (BMRB) UK population estimates*

Annual household income	Prima home workers (%)	Prima readership (%)	National population estimate (%)
Not stated	5.2	17.6	23.9
£5,000 or less	5.2	12.1	19.2
£5–7,999	– ⎫	7.9 ⎫	9.5 ⎫
£5–9,999	12.9 ⎪	– ⎪	– ⎪
£8–10,999	– ⎬ 34.5	12.1 ⎬ 35.6	10.2 ⎬ 30.8
£10–14,999	21.6 ⎪	– ⎪	– ⎪
£11–14,999	– ⎭	15.6 ⎭	11.1 ⎭
£15–19,999	22.1	15.1	10.9
£20–24,999	13.9	10.4	7.0
£25,000+	19.1	8.8	7.8

Note: The income bands between £5–14,999 are not comparable across the table, we have bracketed these incomes.

Sources: Prima Readership Survey Profile and UK estimates BMRB, 1990

reproduced in Appendix 1.) In all, 401 of the question-naires were from women and for analytical reasons we have excluded the two men from our report of findings. The summary results of the survey were published in the September 1990 issue of the magazine (Appendix 2). While we did not have time to do follow-up interviews, we feel that the accompanying letters partly compensate for this and the fact that we carried out face-to-face interviews in the complementary phase of the research. In addition the majority of respondents included their name and address in the knowledge that we might contact them in the future for follow-up purposes.

While we were organizing the Prima survey, Coventry City Council appointed a permanent Homeworking Officer within their Economic Development Unit whose remit was to (a) research the incidence and nature of home-based work in the city; and (b) subsequently develop a city-wide policy for home-based working. Having been contacted by the officer, we agreed immediately to join forces for our in-depth local research (i.e. the targeting of ethnic minority and other urban home-based workers) in our home city of Coventry. This also meant that we could build on our existing knowledge of the local economy. The officer appointed to the city homeworking post is herself a Punjabi-speaking former home-based worker, who was emphatic that our initial plan for a postage-paid newspaper based questionnaire simply would not work with Asian women home-based workers. We had therefore to reassess the question of access at the local level. Our proposed solution was to use the local press but in a different way: to ask home-based workers to telephone us and arrange an interview. English language advertisements for respondents were placed in the local daily newspaper and in the widest circulation free weekly paper in Coventry and environs. The same advertisement was translated into the four main South Asian languages spoken in Coventry and placed in a multilingual free (advertising) newspaper.

We received telephone calls in response to the English language advertisements, but only two women replied to the requests in South Asian languages. The response by minority women was disappointing but does confirm the experience of both the Coventry Women and Work Programme and the Leicester Outwork Campaign with newspaper advertisements; the latter found that, while many of the white home-based workers in Leicester were reached by media publicity, contact with minority women was only established after the appointment of two ethnic minority outreach workers.

As there was no home-based workers project in Coventry, we set about contacting minority home-based workers, with the newly appointed officer, through community workers who approached homeworkers known to them on our behalf. After a short piloting phase, these different methods resulted in a sample of 30 white, English-speaking and 19 Asian home-based workers, the latter being interviewed in their mother tongue if they wished. All the respondents were interviewed in their homes using the same semi-structured interview schedule. We have no way of knowing how far bias was introduced by these different methods of contact and whether this influenced the findings. The main concern was that white home-based workers who felt themselves to be very vulnerable may have been reluctant to respond to the newspaper advertisement despite the promise of confidentiality. This reluctance would be partly overcome in the case of the ethnic minority women who were contacted through persons they already knew and trusted.

Unlike many research projects where the one-off interview is the beginning and end of contact between interviewer and interviewee, the homeworking officer for Coventry has kept in touch with many of the home-workers that we met during the research. Some of those same women subsequently made their way to the House of Commons to lobby, forcefully telling a packed House of Commons Conference Room about their homeworking experiences and how they would like to see the law changed. Some of the other Coventry homeworkers were keen to act as case studies for the *Prima* article, others have taken part in radio discussions and others have taken up the training possibilities that were brought to their notice. These events may not have brought these women material benefits in the short term but none has regretted taking a public stand in raising public awareness of the home-working issue. They know that they have something important to say.

In addition to our two main sampling techniques, we placed the same advertisement in the newsletter of the Working Mothers Association (WMA). The advertisement asked home-based workers to telephone us for a copy of the questionnaire which we were using in our face-to-face interviews in Coventry. The WMA is an off-shoot of the National Childbirth Trust and its membership and thus the sample is heavily weighted towards middle-class women with babies and very small children. Although this group is likely to be unrepresentative of even professional homeworkers, information supplied by the nine home-based workers contacted in this way forms a useful base for comparison with the homeworkers who participated in the local face-to-face interviews. As seven out of the nine are using ICT in their work we look at their experience of homeworking in Chapter 5.

When we began to look at what was already known about 'teleworking' schemes we were struck by how few organizations had been the subject of so much interest, F International and Rank Xerox coming up time and time again. Our criteria for selecting case studies was therefore based on novelty and variety. As no one is quite sure just how many organizations now have some form of ICT homeworking scheme, we were initially helped by a management consultant whose job it is to advise organiz-ations on developing and implementing equal opportu-nities policies and who was already working with a number of firms piloting 'teleworking' schemes. Using his contacts, we employed a telephone 'snowball' technique which resulted in our locating 40 schemes, 30 in the private sector and ten in the public sector.

We were also keen at this stage to establish a rough mapping process to see whether or not developments in homeworking schemes were geographically crowded or dispersed throughout the UK. What emerged quite quickly was what we came to call the 'M25 factor'. Even though the time of these case studies, late 1991, was a period characterized by deepening recession and unemployment, recruitment and retention of well-qualified and experi-enced staff was a continuing problem for organizations and departments based in and around London. There is other evidence to suggest that this clustering was not just a bias in our search method. An organization called Frontline Initiative was set up in 1989 in an attempt to use 'teleworking' as a method of relocating ICT work from higher-cost to lower-cost, low-prosperity areas, thus easing recruitment and retention problems in the south east. A feasibility study showed that new businesses were tending to locate in the south east because it was perceived to be in the 'vanguard of the technological revolution' and were seeking out already experienced ICT workers rather than training people up (*IRS Employment Trends*, 1989: 4). For the most part, the workers involved in the schemes we studied were well to highly qualified staff (mainly programmers, systems analysts and conciliators). The borough council case study (see Chapter 5) is rather different in so far as the scheme was set up to recruit workers who needed only to have keyboard skills on recruitment.

We were also keen to cover both well-established schemes and firms which were piloting the feasibility of homeworking. In one case we were able to follow through a pilot scheme from start to finish. Four firms in the private sector were studied: the financial services arm of one of the big banks (Bank Ltd), an international credit card company (Credit Co.), a legal bureau (Law Co.) the regional headquarters of one of the big utilities (Utilities) and two local authorities, one a London borough (London Borough) and a county council in the south east (South County). The people responsible for introducing the homeworking scheme were interviewed, though in the case of the London borough all the information was provided by post.

What we hope to have shown in this chapter is the extent to which different methodologies locate different kinds of homeworkers (sometimes quite unwittingly) which in turn has led to a number of very different pictures emerging of the homeworking labour force. We have pointed to the more obvious biases that we know our own methodology potentially carries, but we chose our research methods in order to avoid some of the problems we had identified with other research. More open and frank accounts of how research is done are much needed and we hope that our fairly detailed account of why we went about this research in the varied ways that we did will not only help others to look critically at methodological alternatives but also enhance the credibility of our research findings to which we now turn.

3 Racialized Divisions in Homework: the Coventry Sample

In this chapter we look in some detail at homeworking women in our home city of Coventry, West Midlands, which has a population of approximately 300,000 (1994). In the 'good old days' when British motor manufacturing was booming, Coventry had one of the highest paid male skilled workforces in the country. Coventry's car and tractor plants and other engineering works drew immigrant workers from all over Britain, Ireland and ex-British colonies particularly India and the Caribbean. But Britain's post-war economic boom was far more short lived than many of its European counterparts and from the mid-1970s onwards recession began to eat into the city's relative affluence. Between 1975 and 1982, 74 per cent of all industrial job losses in the West Midlands were in the metal manufacturing and engineering industries at Coventry's productive heart. Unemployment levels, particularly among Coventry's less-skilled male immigrant workers began to soar (Gaffikin and Nickson, n.d.). It is within this context that women's earnings, however meagre, have come to play an essential part in most households in the city.

However, our exploration of the role of homeworking in the city suggests that within the shared constraints that all women with children experience, there are racialized differences in levels of employment that force families into a situation where inadequate benefits have to be supplemented by low-wage, home-based work. Unlike white women, Asian women in Coventry were not represented at all in the better paid, less onerous clerical homework available in the city.

For the manual workers in the sample the issues which arise out of racialized segregation are not only differences in hourly earnings but also differences in hours, regularity and the intensity of work. This is particularly acute in the Coventry clothing industry, a major employer of Asian women, because of the extent to which their pre-dominantly Asian employers are themselves in a 'master–servant' relationship in the subcontracting chain of production. Some Asian men may have found an escape route from unemployment in clothing entrepreneurship, but with meagre start-up capital and initially no history of clothing manufacture, they have had to start on the bottom rung of the production chain. This is where profit margins are slim, where the ability to meet rush orders on short runs is imperative and where the most flexible production methods become a necessity: enter home-working women. Clothing production is now the only manufacturing growth sector in the city with around 80 factories in 1994, each with its retinue of homeworkers, but employment in service industries has also grown in the city. What we want to show in this chapter is, first, how closely tied homeworking is to the local economy and, secondly, how the racialized segregation of homeworking in Coventry is a mirror image of ethnic differences in the national labour market for women. We start by looking at white-collar homeworking in the city, an area of home-work in which we were unable to find any Asian women working. While our sample in Coventry is small – 30 white homeworkers (nine clerical) and 19 Asian – each interviewee was asked to tell us about her friends and acquaintances who also worked at home. In this way we built up a much larger picture of homeworking than the interviews in themselves can convey and reassured us that our sample was not particularly biased in any way. We start by looking at the type of clerical work that women were carrying out in Coventry in 1990.

CLERICAL HOMEWORK

The clerical homeworking jobs in the local survey suggest that the supply of clerical work is influenced by the timing of the work, the possibility of firms breaking down work into discrete processes, and the relative importance that market research firms (which are already accustomed to using home-based workers as interviewers) play in the local labour market. Unlike data reported for the US (Christensen, 1985, 1988a, b), there were no computer data entry clerks and traditional clerical homework was limited to book-keeping. We suspect, based partly on the *Prima* national survey, that our sample is concentrated in less traditional and more 'interesting' clerical work than is often the case.

The kinds of work done by the nine clerical workers (all of them white) in the Coventry sample are given in Table 3.1. The telephone is the key technology for four out of nine, and the timing of the work is obviously crucial to the firms' decisions to use homeworkers. For instance, two work for a medium-sized software development firm which runs a contract staff employment agency as a sideline. It employs eight women to keep in touch with approximately 4,000 individuals on the firm's books. They note the individual's current salary and date of availability for work, but this information is later put onto computer records by an in-worker. According to these homeworkers, they sometimes 'chat' with the individuals on their lists, suggesting that they have some role in keeping computer personnel 'on the books' as well as updating information. Most of their telephoning is done during the day, but it usually has to be followed up in the evening in order to catch some individuals at home.

Table 3.1   *Clerical homeworking (Coventry sample)*

Occupation	No.
Telecontact	2
Coders	2
Book-keeping	2
Testing lines	1
Answering telephone	1
Updating maps	1

Two other women who use the telephone have less interesting work. One says it takes a trivial amount of time. She tests lines for a British Telecom subsidiary by ringing customer service numbers (for example, weather forecast, racing results) two or three times a day during peak and off-peak hours. The other answers telephone calls from customers for a local female-owned builders. Two of the other clerical homeworkers are among 80 employed by a large local market research firm to code questionnaire replies in preparation for computer analysis and another updates lists of vacant town centre shop sites by matching maps with recent shop registration lists. Two are book-keepers preparing pay roll data for one or more clients. We also had reports of several other types of clerical homework, including telephone charity collection and looking up telephone numbers of houses in particular neighbourhoods for a firm selling double glazing.

It is usually assumed that clerical homeworkers enjoy better terms and conditions than manual homeworkers, but this is only partly the case. On the plus side, an hourly rate rather than piecework is the norm, even when the work could be paid differently. The software firm homeworkers are paid £2.90 per hour, the coders £2.80, the same as in-workers doing the same job, and even the telephone line tester is paid £3.25 per hour for four hours work, rather than per phone call, although the home-worker says that the work takes only half that long. The book-keepers and the list updater are also paid an hourly rate.

At £3.14, average hourly earnings are much closer to manual hourly earnings than professional work, but they are comparable with women's wages for non-manual work outside the home. Women's average hourly earnings in full-time, non-manual employment in the West Midlands were about £4.80 in 1990, but 41 per cent of women in part-time, non-manual jobs in Great Britain earn less than £3.20 (Government Statistical Service, 1989). The proportion of clerical homeworkers who are very badly paid is much smaller than for manual homeworkers. The only example in the sample is the homeworker who answers the phone for a builder, who is paid £1 per call she answers. (Her rate is not included in the averages, Table 3.3.) Because the calls are infrequent, she earns only £4 to £7 per week.

However, none of the clerical homeworkers receives paid holiday leave and only one pays National Insurance and is therefore eligible for the state sickness pay scheme. Only the women employed by the software house have written contracts of employment. This firm deducts tax and NI for those who earn enough; it also includes the homeworkers in staff social occasions, including semi-annual weekends paid for by the firm. The clerical workers are compensated for telephone expenses and for collecting their work by car themselves, but none receives anything towards other work expenses such as heating or lighting.

Despite the absence of employment rights and benefits, clerical homeworkers' level of satisfaction is comparatively high. This seems to stem from a combination of factors: relatively 'high' earnings for homework, relatively low hours and relatively little variation in the flow of work. The clerical homeworkers work far fewer hours than the other respondents. Half work 9–15 hours a week and none works more than 17 (as we discuss below only a quarter of manual workers works under 20 hours). Most are able to complete their work while their children are asleep or at school and in the evening.

Moreover, as compared to manual workers, their work is fairly regular. Three-quarters reported no variability in hours from week to week; only one of the nine said that she was frequently without work and only one reported even occasional times when the workload was too much to manage comfortably. This is not to say that managing homework is without strain and stress. Clerical home-workers in the Coventry sample are typically women of 25–35 years looking after one or two demanding under-fives at home. As one coder explained: 'My days are a whirlwind and many evenings the last thing I want to do is sit down and code for three hours. It's a very depressing prospect.'

But in the best of circumstances the relationship between the clerical homeworkers and their employers is experi-enced somewhat differently from that of the manual workers. Although some worried if work was not completed on time, none reported serious difficulties or sanctions. There is also, for some but not all, a degree of scope to reduce working hours if necessary. For the clerical workers, household income was higher than for manual workers, averaging £246 a week. One 'telecontact' worker, for example, was accustomed to working 17 hours a week, some of it in the evening while her husband (the best-paid of the clerical workers' husbands) looked after the two children. When his hours of work increased she worried because she was no longer able to fit in 'her hours'. But when she eventually asked for fewer hours, the firm, she says, was happy to agree, saying that she could increase her workload again when circumstances permitted.

A key feature of some clerical work, we think, is that firms have ways of controlling work and work flow which avoid the kinds of pressures pieceworkers experience. For instance, the telecontact worker reported that because the supervisor used to do the work herself she knew whether or not they were reporting their hours correctly. But she still saw the relationship with the employer as involving considerable trust.

There are, however, a number of contrary examples. The market research firm is less relaxed in its treatment of homeworkers, perhaps partly because deadlines are more important in this type of work. We were told, for instance, that although its homeworkers have no contracts of employment, one worker who obtained alternative work gave notice and was threatened with legal action. Clerical workers also sometimes report a high degree of pressure. One of the book-keepers, a divorcee on a low income, reported that she was expected to prepare pay roll data for her employer overnight.

In the Coventry clerical sample, although hourly earnings were higher than for manual work, there was a considerable spread in terms and conditions of work, depending on the particular employer. The economic circumstances of these homeworkers, however, enabled them to exercise a modicum of choice. A few made a positive decision to work at home rather than go out to work. More usually, however, having decided to look after their children at home they then began to look for a source of earnings. Most appeared to be in a position to turn down very poorly paid work; as one said, 'I wouldn't do it if I felt I was being skimped.' The story for most manual homeworkers in Coventry was very different.

MANUAL HOMEWORK

As in the case of clerical work, it appears that the nature of the local economy is extremely important in shaping the type of manual homework being carried out in Coventry. We discovered some homeworking occupations in Coventry which have not been mentioned by other local surveys and vice versa. To reiterate, the distribution of occupations in our sample partly reflects the fact that clothing production is the only manufacturing growth sector in the West Midlands, with a predominantly Asian

Table 3.2   *Manual homeworking (Coventry sample)*

Occupation	No.
Sewing machinists	15
Knitting machinists	4
Bow-makers	4
Cracker-makers	3
Dress-makers	3
Child-minders	3
Electrical assembly	2
Painting	1
Handknitting	1
Alterations	1
Deburring	1
Packing	1
Ironing	1

female labour force estimated at some 20,000 (Phizacklea, 1990).

For the 40 manual homeworkers (see Table 3.2) tasks were divided between clothing production, including the assembly of pre-cut garments, hand and machine knitting, dress-making and alterations and other forms of assembly and packing; there was also one who took in ironing for private customers. We also included three child-minders in the manual group.

Manual homework in Coventry is sharply divided along ethnic lines. All the clothing assembly is done by Asian women. Fifteen of the 19 Asian homeworkers either assemble whole garments or stitch and attach pieces, such as collars and cuffs. Although the minimum rate for machining set by the Wages Council for the clothing industry was £2.10 in 1990, hourly earnings varied between 75p and £3.50 per hour and only one-fifth earns as much as the Wages Council rate. One Asian woman is a dress-maker, with hourly earnings at £1.28 no higher than many machinists. The work of the other Asian home-workers is even more poorly paid. Two assemble

Christmas crackers for 8–16 pence per hour, one packs paper nappies for 53p per hour, and one is a child-minder charging only 33p per hour for each child.

The white manual homeworkers in the sample are spread over a larger range of occupations. Some also work in the clothing industry, but for different firms and doing different work. For instance, one assembles aprons and other kitchen gift items for a firm which markets its own goods rather than acts as a subcontractor. Four make ribbon bows used for knickers and bras and/or attach seed pearls or rosettes to completed bows. This firm is now part of an American multi-national and employs at least 35 homeworkers in Coventry and elsewhere. Most of the women who have worked for the firm for some time use antiquated bow-making machines, and can earn up to £1.44 an hour, although new recruits who are not as fast may earn much less. According to one of the homeworkers, because these machines are no longer made they are in short supply and the slower workers are under considerable pressure to increase their output. However, the firm has managed to expand production by putting out more handwork and using homeworkers to supply work to their friends and acquaintances on a regular basis. These homeworkers are given the responsibility for quality control and payment of their friends' work and are paid an extra 10 per cent on the work taken in from them. With the exception of the office staff and one or two women who make samples, the entire labour force works at home, and apparently the list of homeworkers was considered an asset when the ownership of the firm last changed hands.

Four women are machine knitters, a sector which in our sample also appears to be completely dominated by white women. In contrast to clothing assembly, this sector appears to be design-led and produces goods for a different market. For instance, two of the machine knitters work for college lecturers in design who have established businesses selling upmarket jumpers abroad, particularly to Japan, for exclusive clubs and at craft fairs. Another two homeworkers work for local shops, one as a handknitter and one doing alterations for a local menswear shop. Two are independent dress-makers, earning 63p and £1.75 per hour, and one is a nurse in full-time employment, who when her ex-husband stopped paying maintenance began taking in ironing, for which she charges £2.50 per hour.

The white homeworkers also do a variety of other kinds of manufacturing jobs. Two assemble electrical alarm devices for a local firm, which involves soldering and requires previous experience or training. These women average £2.38 an hour which is the best paid of the manufacturing work, although two of the clothing assemblers earn more per hour. Another homeworker does deburring, which involves inspecting tiny needle-like electrical components. Two of these women in electronics are married to men who work in this field, and sometimes rely on their husbands for advice on how to do the work. In one case the firm employs only the wives of in-workers as homeworkers, and the husband delivers and collects the work. Two other jobs, painting sports trophies and making Christmas crackers, are extremely poorly paid, commanding rates of 16p and 45p respectively. The two white child-minders, who earn £1.28 and 98p per hour, are among the lower paid white homeworkers.

As indicated by the figures above, hourly earnings in manual employment are extremely poor, and there is relatively little difference in average hourly earnings between white manual (£1.31) and Asian manual (£1.26) homeworkers. They compare badly with women's earnings in manual employment outside the home, which averaged £3.23 in the West Midlands in 1990; even among part-time women manual workers, only 11 per cent earned less than £2.20 per hour (Government Statistical Service, 1989). Within this overall situation, however, the distribution of levels of earnings by ethnic group is distinctive, especially once clerical homework is included. As shown in Table 3.3, hourly earnings for Asian homeworkers in the sample are concentrated in a narrow range; two-thirds earn between

Table 3.3   *Distribution of clerical and manual homeworkers' hourly earnings (Coventry sample)*

Hourly rate (£)	White	Asian
<0.25	2	2
0.25–0.49	2	–
0.50–0.74	3	1
0.75–0.99	3	5
1.00–1.24	1	2
1.24–1.49	2	6
1.50–1.74	–	–
1.75–1.99	2	–
2.00–2.24	3	1
2.25–2.49	2	–
2.50–2.74	2	1
2.75–2.99	4	–
3.00–3.24	–	–
3.25–3.49	2	–
3.50–3.74	–	1
3.75–3.99	–	–
4.00–4.24	–	–
4.25–4.49	–	–
5.00+	1	–

75p and £1.50 an hour. In contrast, earnings for white homeworkers are more spread out across the wages span. The proportion of white homeworkers who earn very low wages (below 75p) is slightly higher, but nearly half earn £2 or more.

The Coventry study confirms what we already know about national labour markets for the homeworking labour force. There is a high degree of racialized occupational segregation with Asian women concentrated in a narrower range of jobs and excluded from the better paid and less onerous clerical work. If they have sewing skills (and the capital to purchase a sewing machine) their hourly earnings are low; if not, they are usually thrown into even more poorly paid assembly work. The earnings of those who have set up independently, the dress-maker and child-minder, are in turn affected by the low incomes of

Asian households. For instance, the Asian child-minder charges much less per child than the white child-minders; she says that she has not registered because at the rates her clients can afford, in order to make minding financially viable, she needs to care for more children than registered child-minders are legally permitted.

HOMEWORK IN THE HOUSEHOLD ECONOMY

Equally important are differences in the place of home-work in the women's lives and its role in the household economy. For example, the two lowest paid of the white homeworkers are in a somewhat different situation from the other white or Asian manual homeworkers. One is a handknitter who clearly does not need the money; her husband is an engineer on an oil rig, two weeks on and two weeks off. She says that she knits compulsively while (indeed because) he is away so much. At the time of the interview the other, married to a miner, had stopped working after she was paid £10 for 8 weeks' work painting sports trophies. The paint fumes affected her son's asthma, and she was quite unwilling to work for so little. She had therefore decided to hold on to her remaining trophies to try to get some more money out of the firm.

While these two cases are not typical of the white homeworkers, they are indicative of wider differences in the financial pressures facing white and Asian home-working households. As is the case in the wider economy (Roberts, 1994), the Asian women are much more likely to work full-time than white women. The white clerical workers work an average of 12 hours per week, to a maximum of 17. The white manual workers' working week is considerably longer, an average of 26 hours, to a maximum of 84 hours a week for a bow-maker in her fifties with only her husband's pension as income. Her children are grown up and she does bows most of the time she is awake, taking along her box of bows when she visits neighbours. The proportion of Asian women who work very long hours is higher still. The average working week is some 48 hours, although it is again a retired woman with no children to look after who works the longest hours. Nearly 60 per cent of the Asian women work 45 hours or more and one-third works 60 hours or more.

The very long hours put in by the Asian women reflect economic need. Although average household income differs between the Asian and white manual workers (£191 and £207 respectively), the difference in average household income excluding homework earnings is greater, £146 for the Asian homeworkers and £184 for the white. Twelve of the 19 Asian homeworking households depend on income support (as compared to three white households on income support or state pension). The number and age of children, moreover, not only further limit employment options, but mean that household income must be stretched much further. Considering only households with children, the white homeworkers have an average of two children, the Asian homeworkers have an average of three, and they are more likely to be supporting teenagers still at school.

There are substantial differences in how the Asian and white women discuss the 'advantages' of home working. The white homeworkers, manual as well as clerical, are more likely to mention working 'to suit themselves' or 'flexibility' or being 'able to have a holiday when you want' as among the 'advantages'. For instance, one white dress-maker mentions 'the convenience of coffee when you want it, you can nip up to the shops, the schools can contact you'. However, five of the Asian homeworkers mentioned no advantages at all and none mentioned flexibility for themselves. Although we are sceptical about the extent to which most homeworkers actually avoid timetabling constraints, it is obvious that for those homeworkers who work very long hours, who include many more of the Asian women, the constraints on the timing of work are particularly intense. Moreover, for them the 'advantages' are much more likely to include earning money for the family and the need to supplement inadequate state benefit: an Asian skirt-maker, for instance, explained that she worked at home because: 'My husband is unemployed. We cannot manage on the income support we receive. The children constantly need some form of clothing or shoes. My husband has gone for an interview today. If he gets the job then I shall look for work in a factory.'

One of our questions asked whether the homeworker was happier working at home or whether she would prefer to go out to work 'if that were possible'; the answers showed a clear division between Asian and white women. Slightly over half the white women (50 per cent of the clerical workers and 67 per cent of the manual) said that they preferred to work at home, although it was clear that most were speaking in the context of their present constraints. However, only 10 per cent of the Asian women said that they preferred to work at home, a finding totally at odds with the culturalist stereotypes of Asian women homeworkers who quite wrongly are assumed to work at home because 'their husbands want them to'. Three-quarters said that working at home made them 'neither happier nor unhappier' which suggests that they did not feel they had much choice.

The difference in the responses is no doubt due mostly to the long hours worked by many of the Asian women, but also to the nature of their work. Homework in clothing assembly appears to be more affected by periods of excessive rush work followed by weeks without work. Asked if they experienced periods without enough work, more than half the homeworkers said yes, but there were differences between the groups, 56 per cent of the clerical workers replying yes, 60 per cent of the white manual workers and 88 per cent of the Asian. All the Asian women as compared to only 38 per cent of the white manual workers (and 29 per cent of the clerical) said that they felt there was a lot of pressure on them as homeworkers.

We also asked whether working at home made for 'an easy-going day'. Seventy-seven per cent of the clerical homeworkers said yes, probably a reflection of their lower hours. In contrast, only about half the white manual workers agreed. The half who denied it made for an easy-going day expressed strong feelings. For instance, one electrical assembly worker solders burglar alarm devices while her youngest child is sleeping, as she fears the fumes will affect his health; she fits other stages of the work in at other times. She looked so astonished by the question that the interviewer explained, as neutrally as possible, that this was one of the conclusions of a Department of Employment report (Cragg and Dawson, 1981). 'It must have been written by a man' she replied (which it was).

Although nearly half the white manual workers had strong feelings on this subject, the proportion denying that homework made for an easy-going day was even higher – three-quarters – among the Asian women. Many described the intense pressure they experienced:

Work is always there to be done, housework, homework. I shout most of the time at the children, my temper is lost very quickly. The children have to make their own tea most of the time. I don't have as much time for them as I would like. The homework is messy and creates more work for me.

My work is never finished. Even when I am waiting for work I can't relax as I am thinking of the money I am losing.

The data demonstrate a strong overlap in the situations of Asian and white homeworkers doing manual work. There are examples of extraordinarily poor wages, over-work, homework-related ill health (and indeed of a positive choice in favour of looking after children themselves) among both white and Asian homeworkers. None enjoys any of the employment rights or benefits of employees and none is recompensed for work-related expenses. But, at the same time, the overall profiles of the white and Asian homeworkers do differ. In our sample the latter are much more likely to be dependent on benefit and/or trying to manage on a very low income; in consequence they are thrown into homework which is so badly paid that they need to work very long hours; the pressure of work (and the additional stress created by irregularity of work) typical of the clothing sector then compound the problems.

So why are Asian women not getting the better paid clerical jobs in Coventry? Part of the explanation is the informal recruitment processes so typical of homeworking. Contrary to popular belief, none of the Asian women in our sample acquired her job through relatives; rather, where it exists, the recruitment of kin can discriminate against minority women; for instance, the better paid electronics homework carried out by white women in Coventry was brought home by husbands who worked in the factory. The better paid clerical homework was acquired through word of mouth as was the bow-making. The Commission for Racial Equality, (CRE, 1982), investigation into recruitment at the Massey Ferguson plant in Coventry uncovered a similar process of indirect racial discrimination reproduced through informal recruitment practices. These ethnic differences reflect differences in the national labour market for women.

RACIALIZED DIFFERENCES AT THE NATIONAL LEVEL

The Equal Opportunities Commission published two reports in 1994 indicating the degree of racialized segregation that continues to exist in British labour markets (Bhavnani, 1994; Owen, 1994). A useful summary of the two reports by Bethan Roberts (1994) indicates that even when black and ethnic minority women are skilled and experienced they are twice as likely to be unemployed and work longer hours in poorer conditions for lower pay than white women.

The marked differences in unemployment levels have

been evident for over 20 years and led Policy Studies Institute (PSI) analysts to argue as early as 1982 that any apparent bridging of the gap in job levels between ethnic minority and white women is largely illusory, much of the change being due to the fact that black women in the poorest jobs have become unemployed and those in the better jobs have become a larger proportion of all those in employment (Brown, 1984: 179). In 1994 Pakistani and Bangladeshi women were five times more likely to be unemployed than white women, the gap being greatest in recessionary periods. The EOC suggests a number of factors operating here; one is that ethnic minority women may have less access to informal organizational networks which may help them in gaining access to a wider range of jobs (we have seen how this may operate in Coventry with clerical homeworking); another is that some minority ethnic groups are more likely to use word of mouth recruitment methods which distance them from formal job search methods. Again, we have seen how this results in ghettoization in the clothing industry for Asian women in Coventry. Finally, the EOC suggests that employers may also be more likely to be operating discriminatory practices in a recession (Roberts, 1994: 15).

Another factor which is important in comparing black and white women's job levels is that ethnic minority women are much more likely to work full-time (70 per cent compared to 50 per cent of white women). As we have seen in the case of Coventry homeworkers, this can be explained with reference to household finances and the greater dependency that the Asian households have on the mother's earnings. The 1982 PSI report provides evidence to show that in all types of household the earned income per person is particularly low in Asian households (Brown, 1984: 231). In addition, it has been argued that while full-time work lifts many white women out of low pay ghettos this is far less true for black women (Greater London Council, 1986: 114). Finally, some industries such as the clothing industry demand full-time work.

The final point that needs to be made is the continuing evidence of ghettoization among ethnic minority women, with Asian women heavily over-represented in the clothing industry (and national figures underestimate their involvement in clothing manufacture). Owen's analysis of the 1991 Census data needs to be treated with some caution on two counts; first, he argues that Indian women have low economic activity rates and lower rates of full-time employment in 'larger cities in the south and midlands, including the Birmingham conurbation . . . Coventry, Leicester' (Owen, 1994: 65, also 90). Research carried out on the West Midlands clothing industry in 1988 concluded that for every factory worker there were at least two unregistered homeworkers (Rai and Sheikh, 1989). The clothing labour force in the cities mentioned by Owen is overwhelmingly Asian, particularly Indian.

The second finding that needs treating with caution concerns the apparently higher levels of self-employment among Indian and Pakistani women when compared to other groups. Self-employment is often used as an indicator of entrepreneurship but Phizacklea's research on the clothing industry (1990) showed what a poor indicator this was in the case of women working in that industry. She found that many of the clothing workers interviewed were only technically self-employed because their employer was not prepared to shoulder the fiscal and legal responsibilities that go with that status. In reality, these workers were receiving work from only one company and were working under supervision on its premises. They were therefore working under employee conditions without the benefits that go with that status. The same applies to homeworkers; many of the women that we interviewed in this study said that they were self-employed, but this was a purely subjective assessment of their employment situation. Nevertheless, these same women did not control the amount of work they were given, how or when it was to be completed or to whom it was sold. Their employer controlled all of these factors.

Having examined various legal tests used to ascertain employment status, one commentator concludes that the 'entrepreneurial' approach tested by the answer to the question 'Is this person her/his own boss?' ultimately proves to be the most significant of all the factors in deciding the nature of the employment relationship (Roxby, 1984: 29).

According to DE longitudinal data, there has been a significant increase in the occupational category defined as corporate managers and administrators over the past decade. The growth in this category has been most marked among women and paralleled by increased earnings (Elias and Gregory, 1992). Nevertheless, when we break these figures down by ethnicity we find that minority women are over-represented in areas of occupational decline and under-represented in the growth areas. While there are plenty of well-qualified ethnic minority women moving into the growth areas, their numbers are still small compared to those seemingly locked into the declining, low-paid, low-skill sectors of manufacturing and the manual sectors of women's work. For those less well qualified, evidence collected on a European-wide basis suggests that those with limited or no skills are becoming less mobile concentrating on the local labour market and the informal economy (*Eurostat*, 1989).

There is a real danger here that the increased polarization that we have witnessed occurring in the United States during the 1980s could be happening in Britain and perhaps more widely in Europe too. While the 1980s saw a big increase in women's representation among the managerial and professional ranks in the US, it was also a decade of savage cuts in welfare programmes. It has been argued that this has led to a further racialized polarization among women with white women at the top and black women disproportionately clustered at the bottom of the economic scale (Power, 1988: 145).

Supply-side explanations for occupational segregation by sex have emphasized women's 'domestic reponsibilities' as the key to their disadvantaged and occupationally crowded position in the labour market. For ethnic minority women, and particularly for first-generation Asian women like the women in our Coventry sample, their supposed 'language deficiencies' and 'lack of skills' are routinely trotted out as explanations for their doubly disadvantaged position. There is little doubt that employers take advantage of these gendered and racialized ideologies (see Phizacklea, 1983). While language can constitute a problem for some women, the last PSI study of racial disadvantage at work indicated that this is far less of a problem than is commonly thought (Brown, 1984).

What is often overlooked is the role of the state in shaping job status through immigration policy. Obviously this is formally the case with specific recruitment policies and work permit allocations, but state intervention is apparent in less direct forms in the case of family reunion. Since the early 1970s and the banning of new worker entries throughout the European Community, the major migration flows have been related to family reunion, asylum seekers and refugees. In the case of family reunion the entry of spouses and dependants is only allowed if a sponsor can provide evidence that he or she can support and accommodate them without recourse to 'public funds' (particularly benefits). Not only is the family then forced to settle without state support, there are also residence conditions for non-contributory benefit claims and in some countries a waiting period before access to the labour market is granted. All of these factors push families, who are struggling to reconstruct their lives in the migration setting, into poverty and often women into work in the informal economy. What is perhaps most worrying is that while all the Asian women we interviewed in Coventry were first generation, they were not recent arrivals. But with continuing evidence of racial discrimination operating in the formal labour market the plight of settlers is often not much better than the most recently arrived.

CONCLUSION

The data reported here clearly show that working at home is usually the result of constrained options. These reflect gendered ideologies which assign women the main responsibility for bringing up children; not only day-to-day care but also, for example, the responsibility for encouraging their children by being available for school events. They also reflect the priority given to husbands' employment (and unemployment) and the long hours and irregular shifts which prevent men from playing a more equal role should they wish. Finally, they reflect difficulties in finding employment which is organized around the unpaid work for which women currently take the major responsibility.

However, within this overall picture the nature and intensity of constraints do vary, producing a range of possibilities for making 'choices'. The operation of the state income support system removes all choice; the women whose households are reliant on benefit may or may not prefer to work at home, but within the existing system the capacity to follow their preference is simply not there. Higher unemployment for black than white men means that many more Asian than white women are constrained in this way. As in the wider economy, the occupational segregation of Asian women is so marked that many not on benefit may still find they have little option but work in the clothing industry (Roberts, 1994).

In general, the situation of the white homeworkers is also constrained, but by different factors and to a somewhat lesser degree. Like most women with growing families, they too need to work for money but appear to have some possibility of comparing (highly constrained) options. A large proportion have preschool children and compare homeworking to a part-time outside job; several are constrained by their husbands' working hours, which prevent them from going out to work in the evenings. But most appear to be able to choose part-time as compared to full-time work.

The Department of Employment has concluded that manual homework is a shrinking proportion of the total, and that because homeworking in non-manual fields is presumed to offer better conditions and terms of work, homeworking as a whole requires no state intervention. What can we conclude from our data?

The Coventry data suggest that manual homework is still more extensive than clerical homework, but because it is not a random sample survey we would not claim that the survey adequately measures the extent of manual and non-manual homework, even in the local area. We would suggest, though, that it is a valid indicator of the importance of the local economy as an influence on the types of homework being done, and therefore of the difficulties in using national sample surveys as an adequate predictor of the distribution of homework between sectors and types of work.

The Coventry data also suggest that clerical home-workers are clearly disadvantaged as compared to their office counterparts. Although hourly earnings are not always very much lower, there are other disadvantages. For example, even relatively privileged clerical workers who have suffered a spell of illness say that they found that not being entitled to sickness benefit caused them serious financial problems. None sees it as giving them 'freedom'; instead, they complain of sitting down to concentrate after a day looking after small children. But clerical homework is usually, although not invariably, better than most manual homework in terms of wages and conditions of work.

One of the issues ignored by the Department of Employment is that all women do not have equal access to non-manual homework, whether or not it is increasing. Homeworkers appear to be operating in a racially segregated labour market over which they have little control, not only in the wider society but within the homeworking sector. Asian women are concentrated in a narrower range of jobs and excluded from better paid and less onerous clerical work. They are also excluded from other kinds of manual work, like machining bows, which pays somewhat better than cracker-making and the other very badly paid assembly jobs.

The informal recruitment methods typical of home-working are particularly relevant here. Recruitment to homework is usually through personal networks, although some white homeworkers obtained their jobs through advertisements (in English-language newspapers or shop windows in largely white residential areas). Contrary to popular assumption, none of the Asian women worked for her own relatives; rather, where it exists, the recruitment of kin can discriminate against minority women, which may well be the case for electronics homework in Coventry, in which the white homeworkers have family contacts. The bow-making firm, in particular, relies upon the formation of groups of homeworkers through personal contact and, as far as we can tell, has excluded Asian women from its labour force.

Moreover, firms supplying manual homework give little or no training, and this also excludes most women, white or black, from the better-paid electrical assembly work. For manual workers in our sample the issues which arise out of racialized occupational segregation are not only differences in hourly earnings but also differences in hours, regularity and the intensity of pressure of work. The greater constraints on the choices of Asian home-workers is paralleled by greater constraints on their suppliers in the clothing industry, who are operating in highly competitive markets monopolized by the high street retailers in the fashion clothing trade. In contrast, white homeworkers are supplied with work for different markets, and these are possibly less competitive or seasonal, so that homework is somewhat less pressured. For the kinds of clerical work in the Coventry sample, homeworking labour costs form a smaller proportion of costs than in the clothing industry and this may allow the supplier to pay higher wages. All the evidence goes to show that homeworking does not transform the experience of paid work in the way that Gorz (1985) suggests; rather, characteristic differences between jobs outside the home, in terms of differences in levels of earnings and stress associated with the hours and pace of work, are simply imported into the home.

While there is a wide range of work and experience in homeworking, we believe that only a minority of home-workers enjoys what obviously can be the undoubted benefits. In the current political and economic climate there is little to suggest that the benefits now experienced by some white middle-class professionals will trickle down to others. The social inequalities which arise from class, 'race' and gender relations are simply replicated and reproduced in the homeworking labour force, structuring women's access to different types of work and pay and conditions. Along with the nature and extent of unpaid responsibilities within the home, these are absolutely crucial for understanding what working at home actually entails.

4 Advantages and Disadvantages of Homework: the *Prima* Sample

What do women see as the advantages and disadvantages of home-based work, and how are these related to the jobs they do? The data from the *Prima* national survey allow us to consider the range of occupations undertaken by women at home, and in particular to consider, first, how they relate to the occupational structure as a whole, and, secondly, whether, as Hakim (1987a, b) concluded, manufacturing homework is becoming a 'relative rarity'. We also consider whether the variety of jobs done at home, with a range of remuneration and conditions of work, is the basis of a division in outlook among the largely white respondents to the *Prima* survey, although we also include some of the information the women in Coventry gave us.

According to the DE findings (Hakim, 1987a), women's experience of home-based work was overwhelmingly positive. More than one-quarter of the female home-based workers were found to be graduates and, when asked why they were doing home-based work, the majority of those sampled listed the advantages of homeworking, emphasizing in particular the sense of freedom and flexibility it offered. Only 3 per cent complained of health or safety hazards in their work and 5 per cent of dissatisfaction.

Even among manufacturing home-based workers, dissatisfaction rose to only 11 per cent. Earnings were recognized as being low, but this was explained in terms of relatively short working hours with two-thirds working 16 hours a week or less. Three-quarters of the respondents said that they were satisfied with their rates of pay and two-thirds indicated that they could control the amount of work that they took in (Hakim, 1987a). To reiterate, such findings were much at variance with evidence from research carried out by the Low Pay Unit and local homeworking campaigns. Indeed, the Department of Employment research programme was a direct response to the claims of the Low Pay Unit and others that there continued to be a large pool of extremely ill-paid manufacturing home-based workers dependent on low earnings and forced to accept long hours to make ends meet.

Since then, Catherine Hakim, though no longer director of the DE research on home-based work, has argued that its findings indicate a conflict of interest within the home-based labour force (LSE Conference on Home-Based Work, 17 November 1990). If we have understood her correctly, she now suggests that the interests of the small and declining number of manufacturing homeworkers and their representatives, who seek more regulation of homework, are not shared by the growing number of white-collar homeworkers, who are satisfied with homework, despite the low earnings, since it enables them to look after their children. Their interest is in an expansion of home-based work opportunities. Since homeworking is mutually advantageous for worker and supplier, with the exception of the declining number of manufacturing workers, there is no widespread demand for or need for change.

Is this a useful argument? It is supported by assumptions of very different kinds. Much will depend on whether or not proposed or existing regulations prohibit waged work at home, or makes it prohibitively expensive for suppliers, or whether we simply seek to bring home-based workers within the scope of the officially enumerated and protected labour force. In the United States, for instance, trade unions in the 1930s successfully obtained legislation which prohibited waged homework in some sectors of some industries in order to prevent in-house labour being undercut, and it may be this kind of regulation that Hakim is thinking about. As Boris (1989) points out, it was partly because the US trade unions refused to acknowledge the interests of women, who saw few other work opportunities, that the New Right gained support for the repeal of prohibitory legislation. Their campaign was symbolized by a group of lower middle-class Vermont home knitters and defined in terms of women's right to work at home. However, in Britain legislation has never tried to prohibit waged work at home, except in certain very hazardous trades or occupations. It is not clear why women working at home would oppose any kind of regulation nor how far suppliers would continue to use homeworkers in the interests of flexibility, even if costs were somewhat higher.

There is a further problem with Hakim's argument, however. A key issue is whether or not remuneration and employment rights should depend on the status of the worker, or whether we should be moving towards an equal opportunities approach in which the work itself, rather than simply the gender or 'race' of the worker is what counts. For generations, men's right to a 'family wage' has formed the basis of their higher wages, while women bear the costs of accepting work which fits into the timetables of care for children and other dependants. This idea is no longer acceptable. Why should women be paid less for the work they do simply because they are also responsible for children? Since temporal and spatial arrangements in employment are mostly organized around men, it is not surprising if women are glad of work which they feel they can organize around their day. But it is by no means clear that they are happy to be disadvantaged by a legacy of employment organization which works against them.

Another problem in Hakim's argument is imagining that there is a clear-cut division between sweated 'slave' homeworking labour and the privileged suburban home-based professional or clerical worker. This is a more general perception. Some of the seeming polarity in the debate around home-based work can be explained by the differing methodologies and sampling procedures used in producing evidence that we discussed in Chapter 2. Because the unofficial local surveys have been conducted largely in the inner cities the very positive picture of the relatively privileged clerical or professional suburban worker remains largely unchallenged by homeworking campaigners.

However, equally important in perpetuating divisive views of home-based workers, we would argue, are media images of home-based work, whether or not they are based on research or formal studies. Media presentations of manual homeworkers generally portray them as sorry victims rather than as ordinary women choosing between very narrowly constrained options. For example, a not untypical article in one women's magazine started its piece on homeworking as follows:

> She sits in her cramped, chilly kitchen, hunched over her sewing machine, forcing her fingers to sew one last seam.
>
> It's 1.30 a.m. and Annie Evans started working 19 hours ago. Her fingers are pricked and bleeding and she's totally exhausted. But if Annie doesn't make up 15 pairs of trousers tonight there won't be anything for the family's tea tomorrow. (*Bella*, 1990)

It is noticeable that when similar women's magazines run articles about working at home as a viable option for their own readers they do not address them as victims in this way, even when such readers may earn very little more than 'Annie Evans'. Rather they point out advantages and disadvantages in the expectation that the reader sees herself as deciding between options. These magazines see their readers as making the best of things and having a positive attitude towards life, which they do their best to encourage. As has frequently been noted, these magazines have absorbed many feminist attitudes, including a favourable attitude to women working, but, while they will oppose unfair treatment, they neither foster nor mobilize a vocabulary of resistance to the constraints posed for women by ordinary domestic circumstances. Differences in capacities to make choices usually go unremarked, along with explicit mention of the external and internalized constraints on women's work options. These constraints are very important in constructing women's views of the advantages and disadvantages of working at home but are frequently so taken for granted that they are not made explicit.

As we show in this chapter, professional and manual homeworkers differ in their perceptions of the advantages and disadvantages of working at home. Women in professional and managerial occupations perceive advantages which manual workers do not. But both groups have many of the same complaints, including the unpredictability of earnings, the interference with family life and others' tendency to treat their jobs as something other than 'real work'. Although no doubt they would not see themselves as homogeneous, there is certainly no evidence that they would see themselves as having opposing interests.

In this chapter, then, we relate the occupational distribution of the national sample of home-based workers to their perceptions of the advantages and disadvantages of homework. We also consider these more fully with reference to the qualitative comments of the *Prima* readers, including the letters they enclosed with their questionnaires.

THE *PRIMA* HOME-BASED WORKERS

Although the *Prima* survey, to which we now turn, incorporates a much larger sample numerically, in some

Table 4.1   *Age profile of* Prima *homeworkers compared to* Prima *readership and UK female population over 15 years (1990)*

Age (yr)	*Prima* homeworkers (%)	*Prima* readership (%)	UK female population (%)
15–24	2.8	24.0	17.2
25–34	45.2	30.0	17.9
35–44	37.3	20.7	16.3
45–54	11.5	12.0	13.4
55–64	1.8	8.7	12.4
65+	1.0	4.5	22.5

Note: Percentages may not total 100.
Sources: JIC NARS, Table 103, July 1989–June 1990. *Prima* readership given as 2,246,000. UK female population 15+ estimated at 23,408,000

ways the respondents are drawn from a more narrowly defined social group than our Coventry respondents. Of the 403 home-based workers who returned questionnaires to us, all but two were women (for analytical reasons we excluded the two men from our analyses), 53 per cent were under 35 years of age, 84 per cent were married or living with a partner, 46 per cent had 'O' levels and 13 per cent had a degree. Only nine of the 334 who responded to the question of ethnic origin indicated that they were not 'Europeans'. Table 2.1 (p. 40) shows that our sample is under-representative of women living in households where annual income is £5,000 a year or less and is over-representative of the 'better-off'. Fifty-five per cent of our sample live in households where the annual income is £15,000 or more compared to a national figure of 26 per cent. Table 4.1 indicates that 45 per cent of the sample are aged between 25 and 34 years of age compared to only 18 per cent in this age group in the population as a whole. What we are witnessing here is the attempt by women in their child-bearing years to combine child-care and paid work in the home. As Table 4.2 shows, a much higher percentage of our sample have

Table 4.2   *Percentage of respondents with children in specified age groups:* Prima *homeworkers compared to* Prima *readership*

Age (yr)	Prima homeworkers (%)	Prima readership (%)
Under 2	12.4	10.0
2–4	33.0	17.0
5–10	45.4	23.0
11–15	22.1	17.0
16–20	14.6	18.0

Source: *Prima* Readership Survey Profile, August 1989, unpublished

children aged under ten years than is the case for the *Prima* readership as a whole.

Table 4.3 provides a guide to the types of jobs that the respondents carried out in the home. They are spread out among all nine of the major occupational groups identified by the new Standard Occupational Classification (Office of Population, Censuses and Surveys, 1990) and include 65 different subgroups. The integration of home-based work across the occupational structure is therefore striking, and there is no evidence for the idea that manufacturing homework is becoming 'a relative rarity' (Hakim, 1987a), nor that home-based work is being taken over by the more privileged. What is particularly noticeable, along with the continuing importance of manufacturing, is the large number of homeworkers doing ill-paid service work, especially child-minding. Although women working at home, like women working outside the home, might be classified as being in the service sector, one must not make assumptions about what this means for earnings (discussed later in the chapter) or conditions of work.

In the *Prima* sample, information on occupation was provided by 377 of the sample. Among them the split between manual (41 per cent) and non-manual jobs (45 per cent) is almost equal. Looking at the manual category first,

Table 4.3   Prima *homeworker occupations* (n = 377)

Occupation	%
Professional/managerial	
Manager/owner	7.7
Private teacher	3.0
Other professional	13.7
Total	24.4
Clerical	
Book-keeper	4.2
Clerk	3.2
Typist	7.0
Sales	2.1
Secretary	4.0
Total	20.5
Manual	
Dress and upholstery	11.5
Sewing	7.0
Knitters	4.5
Other crafts	3.7
Assembly	3.0
Child-minding	11.0
Total	40.7
Other	14.2

Note: Percentages may not total 100.

there is a rough division between those manufacturing products and those doing service work. Adding together workers in craft industries (mostly textiles and clothing) and assembly, gives a figure of 30 per cent in manufacturing.

Relatively few are forced to undertake the slog of mass market fashion clothing machining for subcontractors supplying the high street chains, the section in which most of the Asian women in our Coventry sample were concentrated. Those who say they use a sewing machine in their work include the 3.7 per cent of the respondents who make curtains or upholster, 8.5 per cent who describe themselves as dress-makers and only 7.4 per cent who we classified as machinists. Even among the latter many concentrate on kilts, beekeeper's outfits, goods for horse-riding and stables and other niche markets, as well as waxed jackets or parkas.

The picture is muddied by other women classified among the managers, who run their own design and production companies, but who may be doing a lot of the production themselves. Indeed, we were struck by how the occupational categories assume a separation of managerial and manual tasks which may not be characteristic of the very small enterprises of homeworkers. We should also note that even among the dress-makers, nearly a third were working for a single supplier, often doing alterations for a local shop or repairs for a dry cleaners, so the distinction between the dress-maker and the machinist is not always very clearly drawn.

Answers to other questions showed that the products were well-integrated into a number of different trading networks. Fourteen per cent reported that their products were sent abroad, and 9 per cent that they are sold in high street shops. But other outlets were equally popular (party plan, 10 per cent; upmarket shops, 6 per cent; friends, 9 per cent; craft fairs, 15 per cent; and, most frequent, local shops 20 per cent). (A further 3 per cent said their goods were used or purchased by state agencies, like the National Health Service.) The difference from the Coventry clothing workers, in which production ended up in the high street, is partly due to the nature of the sample, we think, who, as *Prima* readers, are unusually interested in crafts and active as crafts women, but also because, as it was a national survey, the *Prima* sample captured workers in a number of regional craft industries, including painting ceramic cottages or stone and clay figures in the Potteries and inspecting and packing underwear and knitting in Scotland. Other products included jewellery, wedding souvenirs, Women's Institute cakes, free-range eggs, dried flower greeting cards, handmade pottery, or packing a diverse range of items, including pot pourri and herb sachets.

Manual workers in the service sector made up a substantial proportion of the sample. Child-minders, at 11 per cent, were the single largest occupation in the entire sample, and two other women who fostered children counted themselves as homeworkers. Other jobs included hairdressing and a dog beautician.

Twenty-four per cent of the sample can be classified as professional or managerial workers and 21 per cent as clerical. Professional work included teaching (3 per cent), including moderating examinations, and many tasks in publishing, such as editing, scientific journal indexing and publishing everything from financial research directories to holiday lettings guides. However, the higher paid traditional professionals were fewer, and included only one solicitor, three accountants, one statistician and one architect. Others were doing administrative work, including preparing costs for lodgings in court for solicitors, administering memberships for national organizations, and recruiting volunteer charity workers. More routine clerical work encompassed book-keepers, typists, and secretaries to local businessmen and clerks, including two women who worked for school boards of governors.

The answers from homeworkers who were able to classify their supplier of work show that home-based workers are used by the largest firms as well as the smallest, although the bias is towards the local small firm. Eight per cent reported working for government agencies, 18 per cent for large companies and 2 per cent for the national utilities, whereas 26 per cent worked for small businesses and a staggering 41 per cent for individuals or private families. As large employers rationalize and lay off workers, an increasing proportion of the population look to out of the way opportunities; it is doubtful whether such people can be seen as marginal to the mainstream labour force any longer, if indeed they ever were.

A striking finding is the degree of sex segregation, which stretches across the usual manual/non-manual divide. About 70 per cent of the respondents were in clearly female-dominated occupations such as teaching, clerical work, clothing production, child-minding and hairdressing. Even though 24 per cent of the sample could be classified as professional and managerial workers, only 6 per cent were developing professional careers in areas currently dominated by male workers such as finance, computing and marketing consultancy.

A few of the managers owned and ran direct mail services but others had developed businesses in traditional female spheres. Two ran accommodation agencies and published directories of holiday homes, another two domestic service employment agencies; one had started a children's nursery and one a craft material supply business. Thus gender segregation in the broader labour market is reproduced in homeworking.

WHY WORK AT HOME?

According to the DE research, when asked why they were doing home-based work, the majority of men and women listed all the advantages emphasizing in particular the sense of freedom and flexibility it offers. When we analysed the answers to the question 'What do you see as the advantages of working at home?', we were struck by the fact that the advantages most frequently mentioned addressed the work constraints women face and were not advantages in and of themselves. Rather than focusing on their constrained options, respondents focused on how home-based work helped them to deal with them. Although one could and should see this as an example of how deeply internalized women's family obligations are, it is also an example of the highly practical way women go

Table 4.4 *Weekly working hours of* Prima *homeworkers (n = 401)*

Hours	%
0–9	10.5
10–19	21.3
20–36	39.2
37–49	15.6
50+	10.7
Missing	2.7

Table 4.5 *Weekly earnings of* Prima *homeworkers (n = 375)*

£	%
<20	11.0
20–29	13.3
30–39	10.0
40–49	11.0
50–59	10.6
60–69	6.0
70–99	12.0
100–199	16.3
200+	10.1

Note: Percentages may not total 100.

about meeting conflicting demands, one not very different from *Prima's* image of them.

Homework comprises an important part of homeworking women's daily work and makes a substantial contribution to household income. Table 4.4 indicates the spread of homeworkers' working hours, indicating that the mean is between 20 and 36 hours per week. Just over a quarter work full-time hours, 37 hours or more, and 10 per cent work over 50 hours a week.

Considering the hours of work, median weekly earnings are low, at between £50 and £59 per week (see Table 4.5), but enough to be an important part of household budgeting. (Hourly earnings are discussed below.) Nearly

Table 4.6 Prima *homeworkers' assessment of the most important advantage of working at home* (n=401)

Advantage	%
Able to look after children	53.6
Timing of work is flexible	18.4
Opportunity to develop own career	7.7
More enjoyable than going out to work	6.2
Keep in touch with own profession	4.0
No commuting	2.2
Missing	0.5
Other	7.2

Note: Percentages may not total 100.

a quarter of the sample earns £29 per week or less, and another quarter is earning over £100. Ten per cent earn £200 or more.

Sixty-nine per cent of the sample indicated that the ability to look after children is one of the advantages of working at home and 54 per cent said that for them this was the *main* advantage of homeworking. Given that 68 per cent of the sample had children aged under 11 years, this confirms our view that home-based work is usually the result of an attempt to fit paid work around unpaid work, particularly child-care, for which women currently take the major responsibility. A typist working an average of 21 hours a week commented: 'Working at home is great for me with two small children one of four and the other seven, it means I can work around them even when they are ill or home at the holidays.'

Other advantages were mentioned less frequently (see Table 4.6). Just under a fifth of the sample gave flexibility in working hours as the main advantage, which is closely related to the need to look after children in many cases. Only 8 per cent mentioned being able to carry on with one's own career as the main advantage, and the other responses represented only 6 per cent of the sample or less.

Many of the other advantages were mentioned, not as a main advantage, but as one of four advantages we invited respondents to 'tick'; they were clearly relevant for a proportion of the sample but still subsidiary considerations: flexible timing (79 per cent), contact with profession (23 per cent), enjoyable (33 per cent), no commuting (42 per cent), available for sick or elderly relatives (14 per cent), an easy-going day (24 per cent), family pleased (21 per cent).

It is not surprising among the highest paid group (particularly those who categorized themselves as 'running a business') that the more positive aspects of home-based work are most likely to be highlighted. For instance, a freelance advertising consultant earning £200 for a 17.5 hour week wrote: 'Its tough getting started but its worth the effort.' A disabled computer analyst, earning £200 for a 30 hour week, said 'Although there are difficulties, they are far outweighed by the advantages for me as a disabled person with two small children.' And a freelance journalist, earning £300 for a 30 hour week, with two children under ten years of age, had only good things to say about home-based work: 'For me, it is the *ideal* way to work, no office, no travelling, no boss, no stress, no child care *and* I don't have to get dressed!' Such positive views were rarely found, however, among the 37 per cent clearly manual homeworkers, which included dress-makers, upholsterers, sewers, knitters, other craftsworkers, assembly workers and child-minders, whose earnings averaged £1.30 per hour for knitters and child-minders and £2.30 for sewers. They also saw being at home with their children as one of the advantages of working at home but, as we discuss below, complained about the impact on their lives and the low rates of pay.

Looking now to the Coventry data, in which respondents had the opportunity to discuss conflicting demands of paid and unpaid work at more length, it was clear that most of the white women with young children perceived their children's needs as primary, and interpreted the advantages of home-based work from that perspective:

I'm at home for the children, it fits in with school and holidays. If I didn't have a family I wouldn't work at home. (*market research coder*)

Only that I don't want to leave my son. Because he is partly deaf he's a bad sleeper and I have to stop and put him down. (*market research coder*)

I can be with my small child during the day and am available if my older children are ill. I cannot afford the childcare costs to go out. (*Asian machinist*)

The white Coventry respondents with young children did not consider paid child-care as a serious option. Theirs was partly a wish to care for their children themselves, at least in the preschool years, but also reflects the fact that paid child-care was too expensive or inflexible for the kinds of jobs they could obtain, either full-time, low-paid work in assembly or part-time jobs. Even an occupational therapist, who did only a small amount of home-based work on top of her outside job, took her 6-month-old baby with her to work, and one of the best paid clerical workers, a divorcee who did book-keeping for local firms, had found that her paid employment outside the home had barely paid the cost of child-care. Most of the white women expected to work part-time, not simply because of child-care, but because of the time required for housework. They also set great store on being free to attend their children's school functions, and those who did go out to work as well had jobs which were flexible enough to enable them to do this.

To put such emphasis on having a routine which enables them to meet what they see as their children's needs does not make women 'grateful slaves'. It does mean that they refuse to accept male working patterns for themselves. As Patricia Hewitt (1993) says, our aim cannot be for women to start giving as little time to their children as fathers have conventionally wanted to devote; this will leave no one better off, least of all children. The period when children are young is qualitatively different and certain times within this period take priority.

It is important to note that the young white mothers in Coventry did not see themselves remaining home-based workers forever. Like many women, they looked forward to pursuing further education or training when their children were older, and then seeking more challenging work. The irony is that some of those who were older had found this impossible, so that they continued to be disadvantaged by homework later on. If they cannot re-enter the outside labour force they realize how disadvantaged they have become. One former dental hygienist in Coventry, for instance, had been unable to obtain a term-time post in the school dental service and was only able to tolerate continued homeworking by setting herself new earnings targets: a family holiday, new carpets, a privately funded operation for her school-aged son. She had become very cynical about homework, doing it only because she felt their was little choice: 'To tell the truth, the advantages are more to the family than to myself. I begrudge giving up my career. My husband agrees but can't really see a solution to it.'

It is important to recognize that while in both surveys being able to care for children was most frequently seen as the main advantage, not all the workers had young children, and there were other reasons for working at home. Of the *Prima* respondents, women without young children earned more on average than the mothers of dependent children; they were more likely to say they were 'running their own business' and their views were more positive, as they did not have to manage the interruptions children create. A book-keeper, earning £150 for a 40 hour week, commented: 'Gives me time to read the professional journals and I'm able to plan my working day better with fewer interruptions.' A freelance editor and proof-reader earning £7 an hour said: 'It was difficult to discipline myself at first and the isolation took several months to get used to. However its been ideal while I've been pregnant and felt sick for the first 11 weeks. I worked to suit myself.'

THE HIDDEN COSTS

The disadvantages of homeworking were unpredictability of income, low earnings, isolation, mess and long hours, and the *Prima* readers had quite a lot to say about these aspects. Indeed, there were nearly 400 more responses to the question about disadvantages (more than the four per respondent we asked for) than the question about advantages.

Prima headlined our survey 'Does it pay to work at home?' One respondent simply wrote 'NO!!!' in the margin of her completed questionnaire. Nearly half the respondents cited earnings-related complaints as the main disadvantage, 22 per cent noting unpredictable income in particular and 20 per cent low earnings. *Prima* home-workers felt they needed their earnings, at least as much as the other readers going out to work. Forty-eight per cent of the home-based sample said they spent some of their earnings on household expenses, while an earlier publisher's market survey of *Prima* readers as a whole indicated that 58 per cent of the readership worked in order to contribute to household expenses. In other words, a fairly similar proportion of the home-based sample as other *Prima* readers look to paid work to meet household needs. It is not therefore surprising that they complain about the level and security of earnings.

The *Prima* sample had average earnings of £3.40 an hour ranging from 13p an hour to £18.75. Table 4.7 indicates that the higher earners cluster among the professionals and managers. The 24 per cent classified as managers, owners, teachers and other professionals averaged between £6.20 and £6.60 an hour, not large earnings for their qualifications. The 37 per cent classified as manual workers, including dress-makers, upholsterers, sewers,

Table 4.7 *Hourly earnings of Prima homeworkers by occupation* (n = 319)

Hourly earnings (p)	Manager/ owner	Professional	Technical	Clerical	Crafts	Services	Sales	Operatives	Other
0–49	1		1		9	1		2	
50–99	2	1		1	10	6		1	
100–149	2		1	6	17	23	1	4	
150–199			3	4	12	6		2	
200–299	6	1	2	15	26	9	5	1	1
300–349	1	3	2	8	6	1	1		
350–399				8	5			1	
400–449				7	8		1		
450–499	2		1	3					
500–549	1	2	8	7					
550–699	2	3	2	1					
600+	11	11	19	9	2		1		
Total	28	21	39	69	95	46	9	11	1

knitters and other craft workers, averaged much less, for example £1.30 per hour for knitters and child-minders and £2.30 for sewers.

Fifty-seven per cent of the sample earned less than £3.00 an hour. The poorest paid are the child-minders, sewers, knitters and assorted jobs such as a woman who paints porcelain cottages sold in department stores: 'I earned less than 50p an hour. I was told experienced painters could earn £30 to £50 a week – they must have been painting in their sleep. It was not so much the low pay but the feeling of being exploited that bothered me.' A hand-knitter for a Covent Garden based designer, whose work was judged to be 'export standard' and yet who earned a mere £7 for a 30 hour week, had this to say about her pay rates: 'It's something I have to do to make living a little easier especially now with the poll tax. But the hours are very long with complicated knitting and the pay is really incredibly little.' An electrical component assembler earning an average of £11 for a 55–60 hour week claimed that: 'Firms have a captive work force so they can pay very little. If we had more rights we would have less work, so its Catch 22.' Another assembler of electrical circuits pointed to the hidden unpaid time involved in a job which in theory pays £1.20 an hour: 'I have just given this job up after working for them for 10 years as the pay is so low. I was repeatedly going up to the factory for extra parts, it took two hours to get to the factory and back.' The homeworkers for this particular firm also had to buy their own screwdrivers and pliers.

Many respondents were aware of the retail price of the goods that they manufactured, an overlocker earning £120 for an 80 hour week listed the chain stores which sold the dresses she made: 'They are bad rates of pay for piece work. Items sell for £40 plus but I get paid 40p a dress. It is very dusty work which causes asthma, allergies, bad chests and coughs.' Whether or not they were independent or worked for a supplier, dress-makers and upholsterers hated seeing their skills undersold:

I have to work very hard to make a decent wage. Even though I'm full-time I don't get the same wage as the girls in the factory. (*45 hours for £80, makes festoon and Austrian blinds, one supplier*)

Because you work from home people expect to pay less for the product you have made, although it is made to a high standard. (*sewing curtains, blinds and rag dolls, 15 hours, £25 per week*)

People take you for granted, and expect the work for next to nothing.

People still regard dress-makers as a 'cheap' source of clothes instead of skilled people.

The resentment at being undervalued was also very strong in some of the comments made by child-minders:

Very lonely work and hard work. Very poorly paid, often dealing with distressed children. (*child-minder paid by local social services in Devon*)

The work led to a breakdown and I've now been unemployed for a year. (*child-minder in Cornwall*)

Those with higher hourly earnings also complained about the level of earnings but were more likely to resent the unpredictability of earnings. For instance, a computer data entry clerk complained: 'I am paid piecework therefore no work, no pay; this is the most frustrating thing about it.' A computer analyst commented on her 'peculiar contract'. 'Contract says I must work 37 hours if supplied with work, but I am not guaranteed to be supplied with 37 hours worth of work.' And a computer data entry clerk noted: 'My work is very unpredictable. I could work 30 hours one week and then do nothing for two weeks.' Indeed, there was a strong sense that even when home-based work was sought after, the suppliers and customers took advantage. A computer programmer with a small baby wrote: 'Homeworking was not done before by my employers. It was a fight even to get them to consider it. However, conditions of employment are different and in my opinion unfair.'

When we asked respondents to list up to four disadvantages, the responses covered more factors than simply earnings. Although unpredictable and low earnings came top of the list (65 per cent and 45 per cent respectively), other important factors cited were mess and inconvenience (42 per cent), isolation (38 per cent), little opportunity for career development (25 per cent) and long hours (28 per cent). A third of the respondents worked over 35 hours a week (up to 112 hours in one case).

AN EASY-GOING DAY?

It is important to recognize that, although working at home makes it possible to look after children at the same time, it doesn't make it *easy*. Allen and Wolkowitz (1987a) cite a Department of Employment survey (Cragg and Dawson, 1981) which concluded that working at home made for 'an easy-going day'. When we asked our respondents about their day they had a number of different responses. Among the disadvantages cited by *Prima* respondents, 32 per cent complained that they couldn't forget or get away from their work and 31 per cent complained of a stressful day. Nearly half the sample said either that their family resented their work or that it interfered with family life, or both, thereby challenging the idea that working at home is ideal for women with families. One informant (who did clothing alterations for a small firm) said that working at home was 'much harder than going out to work especially if one has to look after children. Strong self-discipline is required.' Another, an aerobics teacher, said that it is 'difficult to balance children and work responsibilities or keep money separate from housekeeping'.

The problem of trying to combine home-based work and domestic responsibilities can result for some in severe problems, as an ex-clothing assembly worker recounts in the following extracts from her letter. Because this letter illustrates graphically the contradictions and problems of home-based work, we quote from it at length:

> With rapidly rising mortgage rates, repairs needed to the house and two small children to look after the ideal solution seemed to me to work at home to supplement my husband's wages. I saw an advertisement in the local press for home machinists . . . I earned £1.50 an hour on average and made £100 in my first month. But the disadvantages were becoming all too apparent. To earn that money I was having to neglect a lot of the housework, I was getting way behind on the piles of washing and ironing that seemed to grow in every available corner, and my husband was making it abundantly clear that he was sick and tired of me being stuck behind the sewing machine every time he came through the door while the house got messier and messier. As well as getting on with the sewing I still had to be at the beck and call of the children – 'Mum, I need to use the potty' and 'I'm hungry, can we have dinner now' would not simply disappear just because I desperately needed to concentrate on getting an awkward seam perfect. The phone still rang, Jehovah's Witnesses and door-to-door salesmen still pestered seemingly every time I sat down. And worse still, I found that because I was 'at home' friends and relatives 'especially the in-laws' completely disregarded the fact that I was actually trying to *work* and were forever calling round for coffee and a chat or see the children, and I felt obliged to stop and put the kettle on. Then I would have to spend most of the evening behind the machine making up for lost time. Gradually I was getting more and more depressed . . . then on top of all this the orders for the clothes became erratic and while one week I would have 40 hours of work to do I might get none at all for the next fortnight, so that the income was irregular and unreliable. This further added to the money worries that had started the whole affair. When I found myself lashing out and screaming at the children, or sobbing hysterically at them to leave me alone if they tried to get on my lap, I finally went to the doctor and I gave up home-working. It had created more problems than it solved for me.
>
> Obviously working at home does suit many many people well, but not everyone; it very nearly drove me to a nervous breakdown! It can be a perfect solution to some, but in many

cases it is just exploitation of people who cannot go to work outside the home. It must also be held in some proportion responsible for undermining efforts to put pressure on the government to ensure the provision of far more proper, affordable preschool care for children and on industry to make sensible allowances that help Mums to be able to go out to work.

Other disadvantages became apparent in answer to other questions on the *Prima* questionnaire. For instance, we asked whether the work at home caused health or safety problems: eye-strain, headaches or backache, breathing problems, or minor or major injuries, and 57 per cent of the sample said yes. This is a very high proportion for such a relatively privileged sample, very much higher than the 3 per cent reported by the Department of Employment as suffering health or safety hazards. It accords with growing awareness of the problems white-collar workers can encounter, especially if, as may well be the case with homeworkers, they have inappropriate work stations, poor lighting and poor seating arrangements. In the Coventry survey, where we could see where and how people worked, it was clear that many women did not have space for (or could not afford) to create a proper working environment. Women making bows by hand sat in deep upholstered sitting room armchairs, for instance; dress-makers only came to realize after some time to try to avoid working with dark colours after dark. One organizer of holiday schemes we met in a pilot interview had worked for nearly ten years on a stool at her kitchen worktop, and not surprisingly suffered from backache. Even when homeworkers do not suffer serious injury they experience the same or similar physical stress as those going out to work, and sometimes more.

'WELL IT'S NOT REAL WORK IS IT?'

When asked for further comments about their experience of home-based work at the end of the questionnaire, more than half of those who responded raised the problem of their work not being taken seriously. Let us take the example of Mrs. T, who runs her own contract cleaning company and earns an average of £550 a week for a 32.5 hour week (one of the highest earners in the *Prima* sample).

> I have found that my credibility as a business woman is diminished by the fact that I have my office at home. Friends (both male and female) look upon my business as a hobby despite the fact that it is remarkably successful with a profit level which matches my husband's salary. I am plagued by salesmen etc. who both call and telephone and find it difficult to accept that I am working and not perhaps watching daytime soaps or whatever. I don't tell clients and customers that I work from home, again there is a credibility problem. The children have had to learn that nothing, but nothing, is to interrupt me when I'm on the telephone.

A dress-maker, earning £27.50 for a 15 hour week, commented: 'People won't leave me alone, phoning or visiting when I'm trying to work.' A machine knitter earning £140 for a 48 hour week echoed these sentiments: 'Friends and neighbours tend not to take your work seriously, not respecting your working hours and just dropping in for a chat and coffee every day. Its a difficult situation!'

> People don't always understand that my work is necessary and tend to ask me to do things just because I'm at home. (*machine knitter earning £33 for a 22.5 hour week*)

> Not considered 'real' work by others. (*machine knitter earning £20 for a 45 hour week*)

> The job is not taken seriously. People think it is an easy way to sit at home all day and earn money. You get taken for granted sometimes too. (*child-minder earning £70 for a 50 hour week*)

Child-minding is not generally regarded as 'work'. I consider myself as having a full-time job, providing a valuable service and doing something I enjoy. (*child-minder earning £50 for a 55 hour week*)

AN ENTERPRISE CULTURE?

At the time we were conducting the *Prima* survey there was a lot of discussion in the press about the need to develop a richer 'enterprise culture' in Britain (Keat and Abercrombie, 1991) and practical measures were introduced, like Enterprise Allowance, to encourage people to take up self-employment. We were very interested in whether or not our respondents felt themselves to be part of these apparent developments, or indeed whether it was possible to distinguish 'new entrepreneurs' (Leighton and Felstead, 1992) from other homeworkers. In part, this overlaps with another question which has been seen as a key issue in homeworking policy discussions: what proportion of homeworkers are 'disguised' waged workers and what proportion are more typically self-employed and/or trading on their own account. The implication has usually been that the self-employed are more likely to be entrepreneurial white-collar workers and better off than the homeworker earning piecework wages.

Teasing out differences among homeworkers based on their employment status is no easy matter. We found it difficult to address this question partly because of the shortage of space on the one-page questionnaire which meant that we had to limit questions on employment status and these did not work as well as we had hoped. But there are substantive reasons also why employment status may not be a very good guide to privilege among women. The 1980s is reputed to have seen a rapid rise in low-income, self-employment, especially among women, with most of the new entrants working at home. One of the indications of low income is the gross income reported by the self-employed for tax purposes, and another is the

Table 4.8   *Number of firms supplying work*
to Prima *homeworkers* (n = 401)

Suppliers	Workers	
	No.	%
1	141	35
2+	149	37
Not stated	111	28

substantial proportion of those who claim in-work family
credit benefits who are self-employed (Boden and Corden,
1994). Women's homework occupations also cover a wide
range, with the self-employed including both the teacher
and the child-minder. Generally speaking, our data
suggest that homeworkers who are treated as employees,
with the rights and benefits of employees, do better than
the much more widely defined group of self-employed.

Hakim (1987b, 1988) suggests that a useful way to distinguish entrepreneurs from other self-employed workers
is the number of suppliers for whom they work. The
proportion of *Prima* home-based workers who work for
one or for two or more suppliers is shown in Table 4.8. Of
the total sample, roughly a third reported that they
worked for one supplier and another third for two or more
firms. When we asked about employment status among
those working for one supplier, the clerical workers were
much more likely than manual workers to say that they
were treated like employees, a finding which coincides
with the Coventry data. The remainder of the sample did
not answer this question, but their response to other
questions suggests that they were making craft articles for
sale to private customers (often friends and acquaintances)
or providing a service to individuals rather than firms and
therefore for some purposes should also be considered
self-employed, and in some cases (very small-scale)
entrepreneurs.

When those working for one organization are compared

Table 4.9   *Number of suppliers of* Prima *homeworkers by occupation*

Occupation	1	2+
Professional/managerial	16.2	28.8
Clerical	28.4	13.1
Sales	4.3	1.2
Manual	36.3	26.2
Child-minders	2.8	15.4
Other	12.1	15.4

Note: Percentages may not total 100.

with the others, no very great differences are apparent. The occupational distribution is somewhat different (Table 4.9), but hourly earnings are fairly similar, at £3.15 for those working for one supplier and £3.53 for the others. In other words, *Prima* readers working on their own account, rather than for a single supplier, are earning very little more than the others. This is partly because those not working for a single firm include child-minders and others who are located in very poorly paid women's work. But it suggests that for women home-based self-employment is not the road to riches. Moreover, the respondents to the survey had been unable to benefit from state help for the self-employed. Only 7 per cent of the total *Prima* sample reported receiving advice, loans or enterprise allowance. This suggests that one should be wary of unwarranted assumptions about the relationship between self-employment and 'enterprise culture' for women.

However, when we asked whether the respondent was considered an employee, self-employed or running her own business, a different pattern emerged, in which those running their own businesses were clearly earning more money; median earnings were £50 a week more than for the rest of the sample. But running a business is partly a subjective definition and it is likely that only the higher earners would see their work in this light.

Another surprising comparison of employees and the

self-employed comes if we look at the women who responded to the small Working Mothers Association survey mentioned in Chapter 2. What was interesting here was that the seven highest paid of the nine in the survey, who earn more than almost all of the *Prima* sample, were employees, some of multi-national firms. Four had followed their maternity leave with a period of working from home for a year or two when their new babies were small, but had retained the very favourable terms and conditions of work of their in-work contracts, including membership in private pension schemes.

Interestingly enough, manual workers too appear to earn more if they are former in-workers working at home. In their case, too, local data from West Yorkshire (West Yorkshire Homeworking Group, 1990) suggests that former in-workers are paid about the same piecework rates as they earned as in-workers, although as home-workers they lose some rights and benefits, such as holiday and sick pay. Former in-workers were also much more likely than other manual homeworkers to have contracts of employment.

The Coventry respondents also presented some interesting insights into the role of enterprise culture for them. For them it is not possible to assume that there is a strong streak of individualism among the self-employed, whereas workers choosing conventional employment tend to hold collectivist values (Hakim, 1988). Since it is often difficult for homeworkers to show the existence of an employment contract, with the exception of the telecontact workers all were considered self-employed for purposes of tax and National Insurance. Of the 49, nine worked for more than one supplier: the two book-keepers, who had several clients, the three dress-makers; the three child-minders; and the woman who took in ironing from several households. With the exception of the child-minders, these women definitely thought of themselves as having established businesses, and their relation to the suppliers of work was very different from the other cases. But theirs were enterprises of necessity rather than ideological commitment. The full-time community nurse who did ironing in the evenings set her own hourly charges, checked on possible competition from another woman in the same line of work and advertised in the local free newspaper for custom. But her business was a second job, started when her husband's child support payments stopped, and was seen as an alternative to working evenings in the pub because it enabled her to be at home with the children in the evening. Another example was a middle-aged woman who had always worked as a machinist in a Coventry car plant, and when she was made redundant was more or less coerced by the Job Centre into joining the Enterprise Allowance Scheme.

A final indication of similarities between the self-employed and others, and a clear rejection of a sharp division between homeworking women based on individualist as against collectivist ideology, came in answer to one of the final questions in the *Prima* survey questionnaire: 'Do you think people working at home should have the same employment rights and benefits as other workers, such as sickness and holiday pay?' Fully 84 per cent of the sample answered 'yes', a figure which included a high proportion of self-employed entrepreneurs. Although a few noted that this would not apply to them as self-employed, most, it appears, would wish to enjoy the employment protection offered to full-time workers, including sickness benefit, and do not feel that they should give up employment protection or benefits because they work at home. Nor would they seem to be anxious to defend their independence from state interference.

Given that 68 per cent of our sample have children aged under 11 years, this confirms our view that home-based work is usually the result of an attempt to fit paid work around the unpaid work, particularly child-care, for which women currently take the major responsibility, rather than a predisposition towards individual enterprise and self-reliance.

CONCLUSION

We suggest that those who view the home as the ideal workplace of the 1990s consider carefully the gendered and racial relations that our study reveals. In looking at the results of the survey in the Coventry area in Chapter 3 we showed that the homeworking labour force is segregated by ethnicity in much the same ways as the wider labour market. The *Prima* survey usefully indicates how far the gender segregation of the wider labour market is reproduced among homeworkers. While there is considerable heterogeneity among respondents, with respect to occupation, earnings and of terms and conditions of work, at each level, manual and non-manual, we see considerable segregation into traditional female sectors of employment. This means that few women are able to use homework as a way out of female occupational ghettos, or to maintain top jobs in male hierarchies. Nor did they have much access to the assistance offered to the self-employed by state employment policy. We realize that this finding is influenced partly by the nature of our sample, as the readers of *Prima* seem to be particularly interested in traditional female crafts; a survey of, say, *Cosmopolitan* or *Options* readers might give a different picture. None the less, it is signficant that such a substantial proportion of homeworkers are involved in micro-enterprises of fairly traditional kinds. This group is usually discussed, if at all, under the rubric of self-employment rather than homework, and tends to be ignored when the debate polarizes around images of sweated outworkers and glamorous 'teleworkers'.

Looking closely at the results of our national survey of homeworking also demonstrates that the advantages cited for homework partly reflect differences in occupations, whereas perceptions of the disadvantages are more widely shared. The most widely cited benefit, being able to care for children at home, was far more important than all the others, followed by the flexibility that working at home allowed. Other advantages were cited by only about one-quarter of the respondents. This is because some women had been able to establish work at home which gave them job satisfaction; these women were less likely to have dependent children, suggesting that for them working at home resulted more from choices about occupation or self-employment than the constraints of women's parenting roles. On the other hand, there were more responses to the question about disadvantages than advantages. And the disadvantages, including low or unpredictable earnings and the perception of work-related health problems, were more widely shared. The respondents also seemed to share some of the disadvantages of working in domestic space, including the inconvenience and even resentment home-workers felt their families experienced. Even in this relatively privileged sample, therefore, our findings contrast with the Department of Employment survey, which argued that only a bare 5 per cent felt dissatisfied. There is no reason to believe that among this largely white sample considerable difference in employment terms and conditions lead women to feel that their interests conflict, and their overwhelming support for employment rights and benefits for homeworkers bears this out.

We found no support for the idea that the women who work at home could be considered 'grateful slaves'. Homeworkers' resentment that their work is not taken seriously, or that their products are undervalued because they are produced at home, contrasts with Department of Employment (Hakim, 1980) findings which suggested that homeworkers see themselves as outside the labour force and accept that their work will be valued differently. Homeworkers' complaints that their work is not respected possibly represents a change in women's attitudes towards paid work over the past ten years, we think, as well as differences in sampling and interpretation between the studies. Although the women's complaints suggest that working at home does not offer most women as much job satisfaction as they want, it does indicate higher aspirations and confidence in themselves as workers than might have been the case in the past. If so, it suggests that the often noted stronger work orientation among younger cohorts of women (Crompton and Sanderson, 1990; Hakim, 1991) is evident among homeworkers as well as in the wider labour force.

5 Information and Communication Technology Homeworking

In this chapter we look at whether using information (computer and communications) technology in the home provides the key to a more relaxed, autonomous and better rewarded form of homeworking.

Just as the debates around homeworking have become polarized so too have 'common-sense' images of homeworkers themselves. At one extreme is the image of the exploited manufacturing homeworker with little or no control over her work and at the other is the well-paid information and communication technology (ICT) homeworker who is well paid and commands a good deal of autonomy. This distinction is further underlined by referring to the latter as 'teleworkers' and the former as 'homeworkers'. We prefer not to make this distinction because the notion of 'teleworker' covers as broad a range of jobs with correspondingly different rates of pay and conditions of work as we have seen occurring in more traditional manufacturing forms of homeworking. Our view is that information technology does not in itself guarantee a more agreeable, autonomous or better remunerated way of working at home *unless* the skills and experience that a particular worker combines with that technology are in short supply. Even then we would want to suggest that the experience of homeworking is so heavily permeated by gendered ideologies that the vast majority of male ICT homeworkers will have a different experience of homeworking from women doing the same or equivalent jobs at home. Extant research and the *Prima* data indicate that women homeworkers with young children share remarkably similar experiences of homeworking, irrespective of the technology that they use (Christensen, 1988a; Huws, 1984).

The media have spent a good deal of time focusing on the more privileged sections of the ICT homeworking labour force or waxing lyrical about its potential (see Olson, 1989: 217 for US references of this kind). The media rarely look at the disadvantages of ICT homeworking in the same way that they do for traditional forms of homeworking.

In their comprehensive study, Huws et al. (1990: 10) define 'telework' as:

> work the location of which is independent of the location of the employer or contractor and can be changed according to the wishes of the individual teleworker and/or the organization for which he or she is working. It is work which relies primarily or to a large extent on the use of electronic equipment, the results of which work are communicated remotely to the employer or contractor. The remote communications link need not be a direct telecommunications link but could include the use of mail or courier services.

Nevertheless, the same study underlines the difficulties of this and any other definition as soon as you try to quantify 'teleworkers' or locate the industries in which they work. We encountered exactly the same difficulties in the present study. For instance, just under a third of the *Prima* sample indicated that they used a personal computer (PC) or terminal in their work (though on close inspection of the questionnaires it is obvious from the responses to other questions that some of these respondents may not have actually been using a PC in their work, although most did). But among this group there are cases such as the financial consultant who works for one large company but who describes herself as 'running her own business': is she a 'teleworker' or not? And what about the woman who does all the secretarial and administrative work at home via electronic communication for her husband's business? Both women are working at home, their work relies primarily on the use of electronic equipment the results of which are communicated remotely to their 'employer' and yet both regard themselves as 'running their own business'. Are they 'teleworkers' or not?

We have adopted a broad definition of homeworking in this book and we would therefore describe both women as homeworkers. In addition, our sense is that there is little point in differentiating between homeworking and tele-working: there is simply a very wide range of home-working. In this chapter we look in some detail at why certain employers have decided to disperse some of their activities and adopt ICT homeworking schemes. While we will argue against differentiating what have come to be called 'teleworkers' from other kinds of homeworkers, we will sometimes of necessity have to use the word in this chapter because both the extant literature and the firms that we studied in some depth refer to their workers and schemes as 'teleworkers' and 'teleworking'. We retain quotation marks around the word to indicate that its usage is not unproblematic.

HOW WIDESPREAD IS THE ELECTRONIC COTTAGE?

The reality of establishing the home as office has grown far more slowly than commentators in the 1970s and early 1980s predicted. In fact, most commentators have stopped making quantitative predictions altogether now. In Britain we have no up-to-date national data on how many firms have taken advantage of the developments in information and communication technologies and dispersed some of their previously office-based work to employees' own homes. Even the *Empirica* study which claims to be the most systematic study of 'teleworking' in the world does not provide this kind of data (Huws et al., 1990). Nevertheless the National Economic Development Office (NEDO) estimated that in 1992 there were 1.5 million 'teleworkers' in Britain or one in 17 of the workforce (*Independent on Sunday*, 1992).

In the US The Conference Board in conjunction with New Ways to Work, a San Francisco based resource on flexible work arrangements, conducted a national survey in 1988 of 521 of the largest corporations in the US. Of these only 29 had any recognized programme for working at home (Conference Board, 1989). Our own research conducted in late 1991 uncovered 30 large firms and organizations and ten local authorities or central government departments operating some form of ICT homeworking scheme in Britain. In fact, the increased staff numbers necessary to collect the 'poll tax' in the late 1980s motivated a number of local authorities to pursue the home-based work route. Such schemes sparked further interest throughout the public sector where there has subsequently been a considerable growth in homeworking.

All of the following have been mentioned as factors governing the introduction of 'teleworking' by employers: improved recruitment and retention of staff, occupancy savings, the pursuit of equal opportunities, increased motivation and productivity, response to demand from employees, cost and stress savings on commuting and what Margrethe Olson describes as 'fadism', particularly the favourable publicity an organization may receive as an innovator (Gordon, 1988; IRS *Employment Trends*, 1991b, c; Olson, 1989).

The *Empirica* study argued that an improved ability to cope with work peaks was a primary consideration in the adoption of ICT homeworking by firms in their study (Huws et al., 1990). This study also indicated that interest in 'teleworking' was lowest among managers in Britain compared with Germany, France and Italy. The views of 4,000 managers in four countries were elicited with the most usual explanations for lack of interest in 'teleworking' being the difficulty in organizing 'telework' and the lack of any apparent need to change from the current situation (Huws et al., 1990). In contrast to the apparent lack of interest in ICT homeworking by British managers, a population survey indicated that the British public showed more interest in 'teleworking' than any other country surveyed.

The apparent lack of enthusiasm among managers to manage employees they cannot 'see' is not confined to the British scene. The International Labour Organization also concluded in 1991 that organizational and cultural factors are the major impediments to the rapid and extensive adoption of 'telework', particularly management's concern over maintaining control and supervision. In contrast, the same ILO report suggests, workers have been much more open-minded about 'teleworking' than their managers (IRS *Employment Trends*, 1991b: 5). This raises the question of what actually happens in existing schemes as far as control and supervision of work is concerned.

INCREASED WORK AUTONOMY OR GREATER CONTROL?

At the beginning of this book we argued that the notion of 'control' over work needs to be looked at in a number of ways. Perhaps the most obvious way in which we think about the control and supervision of work is through the external measures used to 'police' an individual's work and productivity, such as the role of supervisor or team manager who will have responsibility for allocating work, monitoring progress and imposing deadlines. Another external measure is the piece rate and, as we have seen, the vast majority of homeworkers are paid only for the work that they complete accurately or at a specified quality standard. The other side of the control equation is the homeworker and this is not just a question of 'self-discipline'. How much control does the homeworker have over her or his work? Again, the answer seems to be heavily gendered. Haddon and Silverstone (1993) argue that the issue of control lies at the heart of successful management of ICT homeworking, but both sides of the control issue need to be recognized. They argue forcefully that

> control is the central problem for households and families. The politics of the household . . . nevertheless define the context in which teleworking is more or less successfully adopted. This household politics is a gendered politics. It relates above all to the differential – but remarkably intransigent – responsibilities that men and women have for their household . . . the experience of the telework, its meaning and the capacity to manage it within the home, are all fundamentally determined by the gender of the teleworker and the particular gendered politics of the household. (Haddon and Silverstone, 1993: 144)

Let us consider first the question of 'external' control and supervision and the apparent reluctance of managers to change current practice. The London Borough of Enfield initiated a homeworking scheme in the late 1980s for its revenue staff. Stuart Dennison, then Assistant Director of Finance, designed and launched the scheme but warned 'Managers have to overcome a fear of losing control. A lot of people feel they are not in control unless they see an army of desks' (*Independent on Sunday*, 1992: 31). This view is borne out by much US research which indicates not only a widespread management fear of 'losing control' but a reluctance to experiment with supervisory methods different from those which currently prevail in most organizations (Olson, 1989). Olson argues that 'in the view of most managers of professional workers, when output is not easily measurable, only highly trusted, proven employees should be "allowed" to work at home as a substitute for coming to the office, where they can be seen' (Olson, 1989: 219).

Most organizations embarking upon the homeworking route now recognize that a different kind of management style is necessary. After months of negotiation, in Britain the Treasury and the Council of Civil Service Unions drew up guidelines for homeworking schemes within the Civil Service. These guidelines recognize that, instead of controlling methods of work and staff time, managers need to concentrate on the quality and quantity of work produced with agreed targets (IRS *Employment Trends*, 1991a: 3).

In the 14 firms studied in the *Empirica* survey, only two relied upon direct methods of supervision. For the remaining 12, supervision of performance and productivity relied mainly on the evaluation of work results as the tasks performed in these schemes did not require continuous work output (Huws et al., 1990: 133).

In practice, there is a wide range of supervisory mechanisms within existing ICT homeworking schemes reflecting the diversity of contemporary homeworking and the range of personnel that they cover. If, for example, the recruitment and retention of systems analysts in a competitive labour market is one's objective then as one personnel manager put it 'we realized that the usual package, company car etc., didn't mean as much to them as their independence'. In other words, having someone breathing down their neck even if it meant a company car was not what those workers wanted. They wanted flexible working hours and increased autonomy, and homeworking is one way in which an organization can provide that. In contrast, the data entry workers who responded to the *Prima* questionnaire were only paid for the work that they correctly completed and had no control over the amount of work that they received. Because all of their work is 'on line' it can also be systematically monitored. In the case of the London Borough that we examined there was a system which combined both elements: flexible but agreed working hours and a supervisor's home visit three times a week.

While there are exceptions to this generalization, levels of supervision tend to be less close for the professional ICT homeworkers in our case studies than for the lower-skilled clerical workers (for instance doing Council Tax bills). Nevertheless, in all cases the employer–employee relationship remains very much the same with the employer controlling the amount, specifications, quality and payment of work, even when direct control is largely replaced with indirect control. Most of the employers had developed guidelines for monitoring work as the schemes progressed. Management of the pilot scheme at Bank Co. which we were able to monitor from start to finish was regarded as an opportunity to innovate and no set ground rules were laid out; rather, a set of issues was to be given serious consideration. The scheme involved 12 lower and middle managers in mainly information technology development. Their managers were given a guide with the following suggestions:

1 How have you or are you to set their goals?
2 Is there some measure of time? For example, what should you expect them to be able to accomplish? Remember they are still contracted to a 35 hour week.
3 How will you measure progress, what procedures need to be put in place?
4 What pattern of work do you require? Are there 'core times' when they must be available?
5 What logs do you need to keep, of equipment, goals, time, results, anything else?
6 Home visits by you, office visits by them: why? when? what for? Is a record to be kept (see suggested log sheet)?
7 Communication, what do you need to do, could you do more, is it necessary?
8 Down time, you will need to decide what activities

individual 'teleworkers' reporting to you will have to undertake if for any reason there is down time on the equipment they are using.

At the end of six months' pilot the senior manager responsible for piloting the scheme remarked 'We've really learnt a lot about management during this pilot.' The success of the pilot scheme measured by both employer and employee meant that 30 per cent of all the organization's head office staff were to become home-workers, swelling the home-based labour force from a modest 12 to 214.

But external measures of control are not the only ones. Most homeworkers 'police' themselves or, as Dennison describes it, are 'high in self-discipline' (*Independent on Sunday*, 1992: 31) and able to work to deadlines unsupervised. The Treasury guidelines on homeworking suggest that the ideal homeworker should have the following qualities:

- self-motivation and discipline
- initiative and flexibility
- the ability to cope with reduced social contact and be self-reliant
- the ability to cope with additional pressures which arise as a result of working in the home where the demands of family life are difficult to ignore
  (quoted in IRS *Employment Trends*, 1991a: 2).

The experience of women homeworkers in our survey indicates that whatever kind of work they were doing, their working 'day' was fairly tightly controlled by fitting it around their domestic responsibilities, the timing of which is often also tightly controlled (school-times, meal-times etc.). They resented interruptions in their working time and the failure of others to recognize their work as a 'job'. Many of these women regarded the unpredictability of the flow of work from their employers as the major disadvantage of homeworking. In the *Empirica* survey the majority of data processing professionals were women who complained about having little or no control over their workload. Given the market power of this group (scarce skills), the authors conclude that this lack of control is not employer driven but relates to the extent to which their family commitments restrict their choice and hence their control over their working conditions (Huws et al., 1990: 133).

This brings us back to the argument that homeworking is a heavily gendered experience. Past research has not looked at matched samples of men and women home-workers. The *Empirica* study was based on 14 companies but we do not know how many were originally asked if they were prepared to participate in the study, the authors merely saying 'after an initial approach to a number of British and German companies' (Huws et al., 1990: 82). Nor do we know if these companies schemes were so designed to retain female workers. What we do know is that the 'teleworking' sample in these companies is 72 per cent female and three-quarters had children (Huws et al., 1990: 59). In contrast Margrethe Olson's (1989) sample of 807 'teleworkers' was based on the subscribers to two trade magazines, one for computer professionals and the other on computing for general professionals. Olson's sample was 84 per cent male.

What is striking about the results of these two surveys and that of Haddon and Silverstone (1993) is the extent to which the centrality of child-care as a motivating factor to take up ICT homeworking varies by gender. Taking first the Huws et al. findings, 74 per cent of women compared to only 7 per cent of the men in the sample rated the ability to look after children or other dependants as a 'very important' advantage of homeworking (Huws et al., 1990: 104). Nevertheless, when the respondents were asked which aspect of their working situation they most wanted to change, better child-care and nursery facilities were mentioned most frequently (Huws et al., 1990: 141). What this highlights is the underlying tension for most women homeworkers, the desire to combine work and child-care but the difficulties in doing so. Haddon and Silverstone argue that domestic responsibilities, particularly child-care, is a major motivating reason for taking up ICT home-working but 'that there is a major gender difference here: it is virtually always women who take up teleworking for this reason . . . most of these women have a commitment first and foremost to this domestic role, and then try to find a form of work which fits in with this' (Haddon and Silverstone, 1993: 11).

When we turn to the predominantly male sample captured by Olson's survey, we find a very different type of motivation to become an ICT homeworker. When asked why they had become homeworkers, the respondents were most likely to say 'to increase my productivity' or 'to work in my own way' (Olson, 1989: 224). Olson's predominantly male sample was not motivated to work at home in order to resolve the problem of combining child-care and work.

Haddon and Silverstone's research in Britain confirms this gender difference. They argue that while both male and female 'teleworkers' complain that their work is not treated as 'real work' by outsiders, it was nevertheless experienced differently because of the 'gender identity of the domestic sphere itself' (1993: 64) which rendered women's presence at home 'natural'. In addition, while most women mentioned domestic responsibilities as a prime consideration for the motivation to work at home and fitted domestic chores around ICT work, men were more likely to prefer to treat the home as a place used exclusively for work during their working hours (Haddon and Silverstone, 1993: 66).

Supervision and control of homeworking is not only a two-sided equation but a heavily gendered one too. But we go on to consider the position of a group of women who have successfully used ICT homeworking to resolve the perceived conflict between pursuing a career and caring for a young family.

MY HOME IS MY OFFICE

Nearly a third of the *Prima* readers indicated that they used either a personal computer or a terminal in their home-based work. The kinds of jobs that they were doing included: data entry (for instance, up-dating mailing lists), computer programming, type-setting, statistical analysis, production control for software company, book-keeping, analysing invoices for VAT returns, market research, systems analysis, technical translation and secretarial services. Others who described themselves as running their own businesses were more likely to be consultants working in sales, advertising or providing trade information or working in some form of publishing.

Some women working at or from home clearly do enjoy some of the advantages highlighted by the Department of Employment. For them working at home is a positive choice, one which they see as successfully resolving the conflict between career goals and the desire to be with their young children as much as possible. Their enthusiasm for working *at* home, however, needs to be seen in the context of the kinds of work they do and their family situations; both give them the space to make and articulate choices in a way which is not possible for most homeworkers. We contacted just such a group through a request published in the newsletter of the Working Mothers Association (WMA) to telephone for and complete a postal questionnaire. The WMA is an offshoot of the National Childbirth Trust and its membership – and thus the sample – is heavily weighted towards middle-class women with babies and very small children. We would want to suggest that this is a group of privileged largely executive women who are using ICT homework to avoid career breaks. The occupations of the WMA members include two systems analysts, one accountant, one book-keeper (with three employees), two design managers, two researchers and one editor. Earnings are high, an average of nearly £9.00 per hour in 1990 and, where relevant, all but one had written contracts. Three of the four women who were employed by the same firm before working at home retained exactly the same rights and benefits, including paid holiday and sick leave and membership in private pension plans.

All spent some of their work time outside the home. They also had some considerable influence on their terms of employment. For instance, when one woman found that she was working 32 hours a week but paid for only 25, she was able to have her contract rewritten on the basis of a full-time, 37 hour week. The majority, however, worked about 24 hours a week.

All had husbands in employment, and household income averaged £519 per week, including their own earnings. They were relatively young, all but two were under 35 and had established careers before having children. They had one or two children at most (average 1.2), all under eight years; five of the nine had only one baby under two years old.

All but one of the nine respondents saw their working at home as a matter of personal preference. Not only did they say they preferred working at home to going out to work, their perception of having a choice also influenced the ways they discussed their reasons for working at home and the advantages they cited. While the underlying reasons for working at home were the same or similar to many of the other women in this study, such as responsibility for children, restricted employment opportunities (in their case the lack of other part-time jobs in their chosen fields) and the husband's employment situation (two spouses also work at home). Nevertheless within these constraints they had made active decisions to reorganize their working lives. For instance, an editor who now works freelance at home for her former employer wrote:

I had had enough of dealing with unsatisfactory child-care arrangements. Good child-minders are few and far between in my area. My 2-year-old daughter was very unhappy at her (expensive) nursery school, which she attended part-time. The rest of the time she was looked after by her nanny . . . Both children (I also have a 7-year-old son) are much happier now and I am able to be involved in all the school and other local activities (music club, gym, ballet).

However, this respondent was unusual in making direct reference to child-care or family needs and obligations. More see working at home in terms of giving more attention to their children at this stage in their lives as a source of personal satisfaction, mentioning being able 'to spend more time' with their children, or being able to breastfeed a baby longer than would have been possible otherwise. This attitude is only possible because most depend on paid child-care, with five out of the nine employing child-minders or nannies at least three days a week.

The other main advantage they give for working at home is the lack of travelling. Four out of the nine still work for the firm they worked for before having a baby, and compare their current situation with the 1–2 hour daily journey within or into London they would otherwise have faced. This suggests that their reasons for working at home, while constrained, are partly the result of earlier (genuine) choices about where to live and bring up their children. They say that it is the time saved in travelling, along with the part-time hours, which contribute to the flexibility all say they enjoy. Unlike most other home-workers they also cite additional advantages which are not directly related to their children:

I dislike unnecessary travelling and city centre offices and like arranging my day to suit myself.

I've got the best office I've ever had.

No travelling, less pollution, less stress, less time wasted and cheaper.

Some of the women have gone to some lengths to obtain work which can be done partly at home. For instance, two convinced their employer, British Telecom, to let them work part-time at home, which they were able to do because of the shortage of labour (10 out of 50 people in their department were due to start maternity leave) and a sympathetic woman department head. Apparently they also cited British Telecom's encouragement of home-based work in the wider economy, and considered their working at home something of a victory over male bureaucrats in the personnel department. However, the one dissatisfied respondent, who was the worst paid and would prefer to be going out to work, organized work for herself only because of her husband's job. She left her job as a museum curator when her husband received a job offer in another part of the country 'which we decided he should accept' but was able to obtain a fee to research and write a book (which she also expects to submit for a higher degree) before leaving London.

Even for these privileged few, working at home has disadvantages; they mentioned isolation and other factors relating to the absence of a spatial and temporal division between home and work, such as telephone calls at unsocial hours or when they are ill. None has been working at home for more than two and a half years so that other possible disadvantages, such as reduced promotion prospects, will not yet have become apparent. Contrary to Gorz's (1985) panegyric to locally based work, those employed by large national firms enjoyed the highest earnings and better conditions of work. But, quite unlike the vast majority of the Coventry sample and *Prima* readers, only one saw low pay as a disadvantage, and none mentioned irregular earnings.

Compared to the homeworkers interviewed in Coventry, these professional home-based workers were enthusiastic about working at home and the richness and variety it added to their lives. While we do not think that they are necessarily typical of women doing professional or managerial jobs at home, their experience sheds light on the conditions under which women experience working at home as a positive choice. Their work is secure, well paid, involves some time outside the home interacting with colleagues or clients, and they are able to afford paid child-care. These are possible not only because of their high educational qualifications and previous work experience but because they have scarce skills in relatively highly paid sectors. Indeed, given the existing sexual division of labour, for them working from home in already established careers may well be a better alternative than the downward mobility many mothers experience when forced to accept part-time employment. Indeed, homework can in these circumstances allow some women to continue a career without a break, ostensibly on the same terms and conditions as they enjoyed on-site. This is also the case for Lisa, a professional homeworker employed by one of the case study organizations.

A DAY IN THE LIFE OF LISA

Lisa is a lawyer, she is married and at the time of the interview she had one 2-year-old child and lived in a large city in the Midlands. Her employer, an organization which deals with specialist litigation, was at the time based in London. Lisa acts as a conciliator and had worked for this organization in London for three years when both a move and a pregnancy raised doubts about her ability to continue working there. Her employers were keen not to lose a highly qualified and experienced worker such as Lisa and were quick to raise the possibility of working at home. Lisa became the first of what rapidly became a homeworking force of 35 conciliators (total workforce 155).

Lisa's working day starts at 8 a.m., her 2-year-old already having been taken to her child-minder. Much of Lisa's work arrives via document exchange and is lodged in a collection box in the City Centre. Lisa collects the work and returns home to start the process of conciliation. Her 'office' has two telephones, one is for her computer terminal the other for regular telephone calls; her employer also provides a fax machine and a photocopier. Lisa makes direct contact with the parties concerned in a case by letter (usually on her terminal which will be printed out and sent from head office), fax and by telephone. The files that Lisa works on are all computerized and about every three days she will bring those files up to date and send them via telephone link to Head Office. Lisa works until 4 p.m. and usually completes this administrative work in the quiet of the evenings.

There is no formal monitoring of Lisa's work though she speaks with her section manager every afternoon by telephone. When we interviewed the director of this organization we were told that in her opinion home-workers were better organized than in-house workers and that this was demonstrated in the quality of the work that came back from them. The organization had identified no efficiency gains to be made in high turnover work going to homeworkers, so that head office and home-based workers were effectively working on different kinds of files, though the work was basically of the same nature.

For the organization, the initial impetus for the scheme was the retention of valued, highly qualified staff but over time homeworking had increasingly become one solution to recruitment problems as well. For an outlay of between £3,000 and £5,000 per worker, highly qualified and experienced staff could be recruited and retained, occupancy costs kept down in high rent central London and efficiency and quality retained.

For Lisa, homeworking meant that she could continue to work at home on terms that were ostensibly no less favourable than head office workers. Nevertheless, Lisa did not receive a contribution towards the costs of her lighting and heating at home and she was concerned that promotion would simply pass her by unless she opted to go back to head office. Lisa's fears are borne out by a study of 31 'professional teleworkers' carried out by Jacqui Cook (1991). As well as isolation, the question of promotion is described in the study as a 'sore point' with some of the respondents being told that they were unlikely to be promoted as long as they continued as homeworkers (Cook, 1991).

Lisa was involved in an *ad hoc* arrangement with her employer which spawned a far larger homeworking scheme. Nevertheless, Lisa now has a new boss with a different organizational style. The whole organization was relocated and homeworkers encouraged to return on-site. Lisa is now back happily working at the new head-quarters, but homeworking provided the flexibility she needed at a certain point in her career. She was able to pursue her career without a break. But Lisa was in a situation where her employer was keen to retain a highly experienced and valued employee with scarce skills, homeworking was therefore a mutually advantageous solution. Retention is therefore an important factor in motivating employer's testing of the ICT homeworking option. We go on to consider what, if any, other factors are important.

WHY HOMEWORKING?

For three of the firms in the private sector the retention of experienced, skilled staff was given as the single most important factor in introducing a homeworking scheme. The recruitment for the schemes in question had therefore been internal. This is not to say that retention was not an issue for the other three cases. South County's interest in homeworking first arose from its potential to solve recruitment and retention problems in the authority. As the financial climate deteriorated for local authorities, so the emphasis shifted to cost savings and the homeworking pilot scheme, involving one whole social work team, was going ahead with cost reductions as a prime target.

In the case of Utilities, competition in the recruitment of highly qualified staff in information technology develop-ment had led the company to explore the homeworking strategy. Over the period of the pilot study recruitment problems had lessened and retention had become the key factor in whether or not the scheme developed.

London Borough was a very different case with the need to create new jobs. Clerical posts had proved hard to fill during 1988. The introduction of the Community Charge necessitated the expansion of jobs and the possibility of separating bulk volume data processing posts from direct public contact with the former being remotely located. Thus while the scheme produced the desired effect in terms of high-quality applicants who would not have been attracted by conventional posts (and there were 915 applicants for initially 20 posts) the retention factor has subsequently proved to be very important in so far as all those recruited have stayed with the Borough. Recruitment for the homeworking scheme in London Borough and Utilities was external and in both cases from the local labour market.

While the retention of trained, experienced and skilled staff stands out as the most important reason given by employers for the adoption of homeworking schemes in the case study firms and organizations, there were many other perceived benefits such as increased productivity (at least 20 per cent) and the 'better health' enjoyed by homeworkers. Savings on occupancy costs ranging from £1,500 a year net per homeworker to £2–3,000 a year were an additional benefit.

A SECONDARY LABOUR FORCE?

In all six cases the home-based workers in our case studies had permanent posts and the same pay and conditions as on-site workers. Furniture, hardware, installation and running costs were all met by the firm or organization. Nevertheless, only two of the firms paid a domestic energy allowance (for heating and lighting). All the firms and organizations claimed that the workers had the same access to training and promotion as on-site workers, but this view was not necessarily shared by the few home-based workers that we spoke to as far as promotion was concerned.

Many of those working at home were described as 'carers', usually the mothers of young children, and employers suggested that 'domestic' reasons governed the decision of their employees in favour of home-based work. Homeworking had also meant that some severely disabled workers were able to pursue or maintain a career at Credit Co.

There is little doubt that in the short term the schemes studied enabled workers to continue working, but of their own choosing to work at home, on terms that are ostensibly no less favourable than on-site workers, while employers retain or recruit staff with valued skills and experience. In the longer term the parity between home-based and on-site workers may not hold: currently senior management jobs are located on site.

All the firms and organizations in question saw home-based work as being more attractive to their female than male staff. When asked why this was the case, a personnel officer at Credit Co. replied 'because women continue to shoulder the main responsibilities of child-care'. Most of the schemes reflected this in their gender composition, although among the professional workers, the gender balance was far less skewed than is the case in traditional manufacturing forms of homeworking. While all the organizations studied have an Equal Opportunities Policy and saw home-based work very much as a part of this, Credit Co. was the only employer with its own nursery. In short, Credit Co. is probably the only organization studied here that is giving staff who are also caring for young children (and this will continue to be largely mothers) real choices. Research carried out by the organization Working for Childcare suggests that since 1989 there has been a move away from workplace nurseries by companies towards a consideration of cheaper options such as career breaks and flexible working arrangements (Working for Childcare, 1991).

As long as gendered ideologies allot mothers primary responsibility for child-care then this will act as a constraint on their employment options. In these circumstances homeworking enables mothers and others with caring responsibilities or disabilities to continue working but in a situation where choice is the outcome of internalized restraint. Even though the majority of women working for the firms and organizations studied are highly qualified and well rewarded, they have 'chosen' homeworking as an apparent solution to the tensions inherent in their 'dual role' as mother and worker.

TRADE UNION ATTITUDE AND PRACTICE

Five of the six case study schemes had been negotiated with the relevant trade unions, and while Law Co. was not organized at the inception of the scheme a union presence had been established by the time this research was carried out. The experience of trade unions with manufacturing homework has not been a good one, the homeworking labour force in the country as a whole is not organized in trade union terms and unions see homeworkers as weakening the position of on-site workers. This experience obviously influences the views of unions negotiating in the ICT situation. While trade unions can negotiate parity of pay and conditions for home and on-site workers, the remote location of homeworkers will make it extremely difficult for trade unions to recruit or retain membership and for the workers in question to take an active part in trade union activities.

CONCLUSION

There is little doubt that 'teleworking' and other forms of information technology based homeworking will continue to be one of a number of flexible working practices adopted by firms and organizations who wish to retain skilled and experienced ICT staff and/or recruit good quality ICT workers who would not apply for a conventional office-based job for domestic reasons.

We have produced evidence in this chapter of what we would term the best possible scenario: women who choose to work at home on terms that are ostensibly no less favourable than for on-site workers, while employers retain or recruit valued and experienced staff. Nevertheless, the material differences in income and autonomy between, for instance, the WMA respondents and the Council Tax workers in London Borough are huge. The technology does not in itself guarantee a more agreeable, autonomous or better rewarded way of working at home unless the skills and experience that a particular worker combines with that technology are in short supply.

6 The Future for Homework

As the [Department of Employment] survey shows, working at home is the result of choice because one of the often-quoted advantages of homeworking is the sense of freedom and independence that it gives.

(Mr Baptiste MP, *Hansard*, 17 May, 1989)

Homework has been touted for its flexibility – but flexibility for whom? This question was addressed by Allen and Wolkowitz (1987a), who were among the first to argue that homework frequently represented the casualization of work, justified as flexibility only because the constraints on women's labour market participation forced many to take on work which bore high costs in terms of low wages, unpredictable earnings, mess, inconvenience and long, unsocial hours of work. As more becomes known about the situation of manual homeworkers, partly through the publicity of homeworking officers, groups and campaigns, these arguments have become more widely recognized. As Mitter points out: 'In order to fulfil her role as a mother and a homeworker, a woman often accepts vulnerability in order to achieve flexibility in working hours' (1994: 16). These more flexible jobs include part-time, temporary work and homework, jobs which offer limited security but which are becoming the majority of new jobs.

Yet, as the quote from Mr Baptiste suggests, there has

been little progress in getting this argument across in current British government thinking. Instead, there has been a tendency to glamorize working at home, in which the manual homeworker is presented as a relative rarity, the clerical homeworker is all but invisible and the professional homeworker is assumed to be a male consultant unaffected by unpaid domestic work obligations. An exception is the recent research by Haddon and Silverstone (1993) which pays particular attention to differences in the options facing professional and managerial level women and men working at home, including the reasons which drew them into homework and the effects it can expect to have on their careers. Unusually in research on the better paid, it recognizes that the homes of families with children are not necessarily ideal places to work, and that there are costs to the families of these workers as well as advantages.

The strength of a project like ours is that it has enabled us to examine the wide range of work undertaken by women at home. The benefit of looking at the full range of homework is that it enables one to see how homework is cut across by the impact of gender, class and 'race' and therefore eludes facile generalization. The emphasis in turn shifts to the ways in which homework reflects all the inequalities of the wider society. Class inequality in Britain has been increasing over the past 15 years (Glyn and Miliband, 1994) and one aspect of this is the widening differences in the fortunes of women at work, with increasing unemployment on the one hand and increased opportunities for women managers on the other, at least until they reach the 'glass ceiling'. As we discussed in Chapter 3, inequality in the employment of white and ethnic minority women is becoming more pronounced. Even when black and ethnic minority women are skilled and experienced, they are twice as likely to be unemployed and work longer hours in poorer conditions for lower pay than white women. Our investigations into homeworking show that these differences are imported into the home and reflected in differences in the situation of women working at home, with Asian homeworkers segregated into a narrower range of jobs and working very much longer hours to meet their household requirements.

We have found definite similarities in the situation of women working at home, in particular their concern with their children's welfare. Internalized constraints are one of the main mechanisms gendering women's work experience. We mean by this the expectations that mothers' paid work (but not fathers') should take into account their children's needs, that decisions are rarely taken with only individual ambitions in mind but involve juggling and balancing acts. But for many women external constraints are as, if not more important than, these internalized expectations. These include the high level of unemployment in the external labour market, the operation of the benefit system, which forces the wives of unemployed men to seek work outside the formal registered sector, the operation of immigration law, lack of qualifications, transport and the absence of affordable child-care. Moreover, some middle class women have the resources, in the form of high earnings, to avoid some of the problems of working at home, for instance through employing nannies or child-minders.

Looking across the data from the different surveys we conducted, there appear to be at least five key groups of homeworkers with different degrees of remuneration, autonomy and security of employment or earnings. Most of the jobs are relatively modest, suggesting not a stark polarity between manufacturing worker and 'teleworker' but a continuum in which the different aspects of relative privilege (status, earnings, employment security) tend to coincide.

Casualized employees This category covers a very wide range of types of work. In particular, it includes manual workers in clothing, both knitting and machining, who work for middlemen as well as directly for large companies (making mail order curtains, for instance, or painting porcelain cottages). It also includes clerical workers with good qualifications with higher hourly earnings, but little security of employment and un-predictable earnings. Both groups are usually defined as self-employed, although the reality is that they do not work on their own account and have very minimal control over how they do their work. Within this group there are signficant differences in earnings and hours and intensity of work and these frequently parallel ethnic divisions.

Micro-entrepreneurs   These workers comprised a substantial proportion of those who responded to the *Prima* survey. As discussed in Chapter 4, self-employment has become an increasingly important sector for women's employment. For some women what 'small-batch production' means, or what an increasingly important leisure industry entails, is dress-making on a very small scale. For others it is building on their existing resources to provide bed and breakfast or organize the production and sale of eggs on their family farm. There are a number of women involved in craft production on their own account, often selling their goods at trade fairs or to friends.

Self-employed professionals   These include independent pro-fessionals, including many jobs which involve producing or processing text in journalism and publishing but also teachers and others who work only for one organization. Income is very variable, much higher among accountants for instance than music teachers.

Very small businesses   These often employ two or three staff in, for instance, mail order distribution or a home-based nursery. A few of these women are formally company directors of their own firm. Women without small children tend to be over-represented in this category, and the earnings reported by the informants are relatively good.

Technical and executive level employees This is again a category which encompasses a wide range. It includes some clerical workers who say that they are treated as employees, although unfortunately we are unable to say what rights or obligations these particular workers are referring to. The homeworkers working for the large firms surveyed in Chapter 5 were all employees, and with the exception of those working for the London Borough were highly qualified and had relatively scarce skills. In the Working Mothers Association survey of well-paid professional and executive homeworkers some were employees of larger firms, who employ a number of homeworkers or who have retained a previous contract of employment, while working at home for some months following maternity leave. They tend to have the highest, most predictable earnings, with terms and conditions most nearly like in-workers. It appears that rather than 'employee' denoting subordination and lack of autonomy, in the context of homeworking it is an indication of status and obligations on the part of the employer.

We have sought neither to exaggerate the similarity between women in the interest of an abstract notion of 'sisterhood' nor to assume that women working at home share a common identity as women. But nor do we think the interests of women working at home should be polarized. The idea that some women have managed to obtain satisfying jobs at home which meet their needs should not be used to excuse or obscure the situation of other women whose position is less enviable. It seems to us that women like the *Prima* readers, who undertake many different kinds of homework, support the idea of extending employment rights and benefits for women working at home, recognizing that it is illegitimate to deny women these rights because they are unable to work according to patterns established by men as the norm.

FUTURE DEVELOPMENTS

What we see as necessary is a range of legislative measures and self-organization promoting the interests of women working at home. We suggest in a very tentative way some broadly defined areas where we think there would be agreement by most homeworking women. A recognition of the diversity and heterogeneity of homework is no excuse for inaction. Rather a range of different kinds of organization would contribute to making homework more visible as 'real work' and homeworkers more evident as members of the labour force.

First, there needs to be a reassessment of accepted methods of collecting statistical data on homework and labour force participation more generally. This is important not only to trace increases and decreases in homework of different kinds, but because methods of collecting statistical data are of crucial importance in defining work and labour force participation, with all the implications this has for remuneration and employment rights and benefits. This is particularly relevant now that the International Labour Organization (ILO) Meeting of Experts has declared itself willing to consider evidence on homeworking (Tate, 1994). While it will be an uphill struggle to obtain an ILO instrument on homeworking, the process itself will help to increase the visibility of homework, especially of the more vulnerable.

Secondly, the single most beneficial measure for many homeworkers in Britain would be the introduction of a minimum wage for which they would qualify. At present, employment status is not as significant as it might be since, for instance, although some homeworkers would benefit, the attractions of National Insurance contributions for those whose work is not continuous over long periods of time are negligible. But minimum wage legislation would have to find some way to incorporate homeworkers explicitly, including those without formal written contracts of employment. It is obviously in the interest of all workers that homework is incorporated in minimum wage legislation as otherwise employers may use homework more extensively to avoid paying higher wages. In addition, specific recommendations for model practice for homework suppliers in manufacturing are suggested in Tate (1993), many of which are already enforced in Australia.

Thirdly, there needs to be support for various forms of self-organization by homeworkers, linked in some cases to locality or occupation. In particular those seeking to establish support networks need to be aware of the strength of feeling that homeworkers indicated in the *Prima* survey in support of employment rights and benefits for homeworkers. This support could come from many places, including trade unions and local government, but also the newsletters and support networks run as a source of income by homeworkers themselves.

Many people will not realize what an impressive start has already been made. Tate (1994) and Allen and Wolkowitz (1987a) document for the 1970s, 1980s and early 1990s the efforts of homeworkers to bring homework to the attention of policy-makers, and the assistance they have received from trade unions and local government. Rowbotham's (1994) history of nineteenth and early twentieth century organization among homeworkers shows that, while there is unlikely to be unanimity in terms of goals or approach, the participation of home-workers themselves in economic organizing is an important goal in itself. Indeed, despite the fragility of some of the efforts homeworkers have made in organizing community businesses, cooperatives and local support groups, Rowbotham is surely correct to set this in the context of the difficulties they face. Highlighting the role of manual homeworkers in regenerating the labour move-ment, she is struck by the way in which homeworkers are managing to defy the fear and despair brought by assumptions of laissez-faire economics: 'Even in countries like Britain where the chances of making an alternative have come to seem remote, the re-assertion of social solidarity against the paralysing attitudes of conservatism which have entered the culture are vital' (Rowbotham, 1994: 82).

The National Group on Homeworking has campaigned for many years to achieve employee status for all homeworkers as a first vital step in their aim to up-grade their position as workers. But the Group also emphasizes that to ensure that the majority of homeworkers have something approximating equal opportunities, many other structural obstacles must be overcome. These include the provision of free and adequate care of dependants, an end to racist and sexist legislation and proper training and educational opportunities for homeworkers.

Some British local authorities, which in any case lack the authority to implement changes in employment status, are trying to help low-paid manufacturing workers as part of their policies on unemployment. They argue that training is not cost-effective unless people have jobs to go to. Since in many parts of Britain manufacturing jobs have been lost to production abroad, there has been increasing interest in encouraging self-employment and in some areas women have been successful in being included. For example, courses in business skills have become an important part of some local training programmes for women (Mitter et al., 1993). These programmes are often based on ideas which were developed in the context of supporting the Third World 'informal sector' and are now being deployed in Europe. Loans to those wishing to take up self-employment or increase their turn-over are an important part of the work of, for instance, the Self-Employed Women's Association (SEWA) in India (Rowbotham, 1993) and AIDE (Association pour le droit à l'initiative economique) in France (Anwar and Chai, 1994), the latter modelled on a programme run by the Grameen Bank in Bangladesh. One reason for increasing the visibility of homeworkers is so that they are fully incorporated in such programmes, and that the particular constraints affecting homeworkers' participation are addressed.

We would expect that there is also much more scope for support networks among white-collar homeworkers. Although this is likely to take place within different kinds of organizations which recognize the distinctive situations of clerical and professional workers, our impression is that many women working at home have been vulnerable to cuts in income during the recession and would welcome help and support in setting their rates for customers and clients, for instance. The kinds of self-organization which clerical and professional homeworkers are involved in, and their particular needs, form an important area for further research. Our *Prima* data, which indicated that 84 per cent of respondents supported employment rights and benefits for homeworkers, indicate that support for employment rights is widespread among white-collar homeworkers and is not confined to manu-facturing homeworkers.

Fourthly, all recommendations on homework, studies of homework and reports to international bodies and conferences should as far as possible incorporate home-workers or former homeworkers as members or participants, ideally drawn from a range of occupations. Many people who have not attended national and international conferences on homework, or who attend fleetingly, will be unaware of the dramatic difference the presence of homeworkers makes, and the ways they effectively challenge the assumptions of policy-makers who have never been in their position.

Fifthly, at the present time racism and discrimination against ethnic minorities is a crucial aspect of the construction of the homeworking labour force. In Britain, ethnic minority homeworkers have been unable to gain access to white-collar homework, even when they have formal educational qualifications or to move into manual homeworking jobs outside the clothing industry. Some would argue that their situation has parallels with the expanding participation of women in casualized work at a global level, including North America and Australia as well as in the Third World, as all are affected by the spread of subcontracting and small batch production.

The main purpose of this book has been to provide an overview of the type of homeworking undertaken by women in Britain and their perceptions of its advantages and disadvantages. We have attempted to set this in the context of patterns of, and issues in, women's employment more generally, as well as the increasing interest in homework shown by large enterprises and their perceptions of the advantages and disadvantages to them as employers. Our discussion highlights just a few of the possible strategies which homeworkers' organizations might advance and develop in the future. The main point is that the framework for considering future developments needs to focus on the projects homeworkers themselves advance, as well as the policies which firms seek to implement, and to ensure that platforms exist on which homeworkers can make their views known.

Appendix 1: *Prima* Survey

DOES IT PAY TO WORK AT HOME?

Together with sociologists and authors Dr Carol Wolkowitz and Dr Annie Phizacklea, who have made a special study of women at work in the home, we invite you to complete our exclusive survey — the first of its kind for over a decade. Your answers will be compiled, analysed and the results published in *Prima* later this year.

1 Please describe the paid work you do at home.

2 Do you use any of the following?
   ☐ personal computer
   ☐ typewriter
   ☐ computer terminal linked into a network
   ☐ knitting machine
   ☐ sewing machine
   ☐ other, please specify

3 What are the advantages of working at home *for you*? Please tick all that apply.
   ☐ able to look after your children yourself
   ☐ timing of work is flexible
   ☐ can keep in touch with your profession
   ☐ opportunity to develop your own career
   ☐ more enjoyable than going out to work
   ☐ not having to commute
   ☐ available to help your elderly or ill relatives
   ☐ makes for an easy-going day
   ☐ family pleased
   ☐ no advantages
   ☐ other, please specify

4 Please go back to question 3 and circle the advantage of working at home which is *most* important to you.

5 What, *for you*, are the disadvantages of working at home? Tick all that apply.
   ☐ being at home with the children all day
   ☐ long hours
   ☐ too little work
   ☐ low earnings for the work involved
   ☐ unpredictable income
   ☐ little opportunity for career advancement or promotion
   ☐ creates mess or inconvenience in the house

- ☐ isolating
- ☐ family sometimes resents
- ☐ can't get away from your work
- ☐ makes for a stressful day
- ☐ sometimes interferes with family life
- ☐ no disadvantages
- ☐ other, please specify

_____

6 Please go back to the previous question and circle the disadvantage which bothers you most.

7 Where does most of your work come from?
- ☐ central or local government office or similar
- ☐ a public utility, such as Gas Board or telephone company
- ☐ a small local business
- ☐ a large company
- ☐ private individuals
- ☐ other, please specify

_____

8 If your work at home involves making or packing things, please tell us where some of the things are sold

_____

9 Do the businesses or people with whom you work consider you to be . . .
- ☐ an employee?
- ☐ self-employed?
- ☐ running a business?

10 How many organisations or businesses do you obtain work from during the year?
- ☐ one ☐ more than one

11 How many hours a week do you usually spend on your work? Be sure to include evenings, weekends and any 'odd moments'.

_____ hours

12 How much do you usually earn from your work at home, per week?
£ _____ per week

13 What do you usually spend your earnings on? Please tick up to two boxes.
- ☐ normal household expenses (eg food, bills, mortgage, car, children's clothes)
- ☐ paid child care
- ☐ holidays, treats for children, extras for the house, etc.
- ☐ personal expenses (things for yourself)

14 Please answer 'yes' or 'no' to the following questions.

	YES	NO
Have you been working at home for two years or more?	☐	☐
Have you had any Government assistance (eg Enterprise Allowance Scheme, loans or advice) in connection with your work at home?	☐	☐
Is the work you do at home your only job?	☐	☐
Does the job you do at home involve any work outside home?	☐	☐
Does your work at home ever cause any eyestrain, headaches or backache, breathing problems, minor or major injuries, etc?	☐	☐
Do you think people working at home should have the same employment rights and benefits as other workers, eg sickness and holiday pay?	☐	☐
Do you use any paid child-care (including playgroup) for the time you work at home?	☐	☐

15 Please tick all the boxes which apply to you.

Sex ☐ female   ☐ male

Age _____ years old

Marital status
☐ single
☐ widowed
☐ married or living with partner
☐ separated/divorced

Education
☐ O levels, O grades, CSEs or GCSEs
☐ A levels or Highers
☐ university degree
☐ other

Ethnic origin
☐ European   ☐ Asian
☐ Afro-Caribbean   ☐ other

16 How many people, including yourself, live in your household in these age groups?

____ 0–1 yr   ____ 11–15 yrs
____ 2–4 yrs   ____ 16–20 yrs
____ 5–10 yrs   ____ 21 plus

17 Please write in your postcode (so we can learn if working at home is more popular in some parts of the country than in others).

_____

18 What is your annual household income (all members)?
☐ less than £5,000
☐ £5,000–£9,999
☐ £10,000–£14,999
☐ £15,000–£19,999
☐ £20,000–£24,999
☐ £25,000 or above

19 How often do you read Prima?
☐ every issue
☐ about 1 out of 4 issues
☐ about 3 out of 4 issues
☐ only occasionally
☐ hardly ever

20 Please add anything you would like to tell us about your experience of working at home

Thank you for taking the time to participate in this important national survey. The information will be treated confidentially and your name will not be used. You need not include your name and address, but please write them in if you would be willing to complete a more detailed questionnaire in the future.

Although the deadline is 31 May 1990, please post your completed questionnaire at the first chance you get. NO POSTAGE STAMP IS NEEDED.

Please send your completed questionnaire to:

Prima Survey, FREEPOST (CV 790), Room 2.51 Social Studies Building, Coventry CV4 7BR

Name _____

Address _____

Postcode _____

Source: *Prima*, May 1990

Appendix 2: *Prima* National Survey Results

Working from Home: Why things must change

Thousands of hard working women pay a penalty because they work from home. But, following the national survey we launched in May, here they have their say about the pros and cons of a home-based job. Report by Jenny Filder

What an industrious lot you are! Our investigation into working from home has not only revealed how many do it, but how varied that work is. And, perhaps most importantly, how strongly you feel about the pros – and more especially – the cons.

We heard from craftworkers and computer programmers, dog beauticians and book-keepers, indexers and knitters, secretaries and artists, teachers and child minders, and some a little more out of the ordinary like a lady who makes kilts and another who puts together beekeeping outfits.

PRIMA **homeworkers – who they are**
Age: From 15 to 70, with over half between 25 and 35.
Family: 84 per cent married or with partner; 67 per cent with children under 10.
Education: 81 per cent with 'O' Levels; 38 per cent 'A' Levels; 20 per cent college or university degrees.
Family income: from £5,000 to £25,000 plus; with 57 per cent falling into the £10,000–£24,000 category.
Work done: 25 per cent in textiles and clothing; 12 per cent in childcare; 18 per cent clerical or secretarial work.

What we really wanted to know was whether you felt it paid to work at home. The answer came through loud and clear – no, it doesn't. The low level and unpredictability of earnings proved huge bones of contention.

But you were also happy to point out the obvious advantages. Most importantly the flexibility of combining work with looking after the home, children and elderly relatives. This came

"The fact that the long hours and very low pay are appalling has to be balanced against being with my three year old until he goes to school"

Child minder, averaging £1.32 an hour

through time and time again, so we weren't surprised to find that most of those who'd filled in our questionnaire were aged between 25 and 35, eight out of 10 were married or with a partner, and seven out of 10 had children under 10.

You also spoke of the enviable freedom from traffic queues and crowded trains (well-known commuter afflictions), from leering bosses and stuffy offices, and of the perks of making money from a 'hobby', of being able to schedule in a game of squash mid-afternoon, or extending the lunch hour when the weather's good. No one could argue with that.

But now for the bad news. Hand in hand with poor pay were the lack of status and rights (to holidays, sick pay and so on), and a total misunderstanding by your nearest and dearest of the nature of the job. Lots of you complained about family and friends who because the work is done from home, didn't see it as a 'proper job', and weren't the least bit reluctant to interrupt you.

Reinforcing this irritation is the fact that contrary to what many might think, most women working from home don't do it for pin money. Earnings are used to boost the household budget for essentials and to contribute towards things that would otherwise be unaffordable, like family holidays. Also, one quarter of those who replied held down another job as well.

Most of all, our survey smashed any assumption that working at home automatically and happily resolves the conflict of mixing work with family life; over half said it actually interfered with it.

And we heard about 'employers' who felt it quite in order to fluctuate work rates, ring up at all hours of the day and even night, and, as one dressmaker put it, treat workers like the little woman round the corner at their beck and call.

AN EXPLOITED WORKFORCE?

Yes, the money compares badly with what is paid in the workplace.

The range of actual work was very broad. Some people work for large organisations — like health authorities, examining boards for GCSEs and colleges of further education, and high street chain stores — but over half work for individuals or small businesses. The finished products — if being made to sell — typically finds its way into a local shop, craft fair or is sold abroad. As many as one in four home workers average only £1.30 an hour, often for work which requires real skill and talent. Stop and think next time you buy one of those delightful miniature cottages in a big store, as another woman somewhere is painting them for 40p a cottage, which works out about 25p an hour. (That's £15 for a 60 hour week!) Another who is a finisher of dresses for high street fashion chains gets paid 40p for a dress which will be marked up at £40.

As a group, knitters came off worst, averaging £1.28 an hour, followed by child minders at £1.32 an hour, machinists at £2.35, secretaries at £3.40 an hour, teachers at £6.65 an hour and managers (of a group of homeworkers, for example) at £7 an hour. Our survey confirmed that *Prima* readers have an educational background above the national average: 81 per cent have 'O' Levels, 38 per cent 'A' Levels, and 20 per cent have degrees. Consequently, we can only assume a broader spectrum of women would paint an even more depressing picture.

But what worried most of you about pay wasn't only *what* you were getting, but *when* you were getting it. One in five of you saw unpredictability as the biggest disadvantage, saying you might receive a pile of work one week and none for the next two.

Of course, those who are self-employed at home and tender clients for work, like freelance artists or secretaries, anticipate this problem. But for those women who work regularly for one 'employer' and are paid an hourly rate, this is a very real drawback. Especially when the money goes towards household essentials (a point you were keen to stress) and is not pin money, despite what many employers and non-homeworkers may think.

"Because I work from home, 'employers' expect to pay less for the product I've made, even though it's to a high standard"

Curtain maker, averaging £1.70 an hour

The majority of replies came from households where there was a total income of between £10,000 and £24,000.

NO RIGHTS . . . NO PROTECTION

Rights and status was the second thorny issue.

A massive 84 per cent thought homeworkers should have the same rights and status as people going out to work, with consideration for things like job security, sick pay, holiday pay and health and safety. This isn't surprising when over half reported that their work causes eye strain, headaches or backaches, breathing problems or other injuries.

The fact is, homeworkers do not enjoy the same legal protection as those who go out to work. For those who work regularly for one 'employer' (rather than as a freelancer for several), this is a real problem. They are supplied with work as if part of the permanent workforce, but are considered self-employed by the suppliers. And because they are based at home doing a variety of work, they would have difficulty proving otherwise to an industrial tribunal.

TIME FOR ACTION

Various organisations, such as the National Unit on Homeworking, are campaigning for protective legislation and want minimum wage levels introduced with full employment rights and benefits. There have already been attempts in Parliament by Labour MP for Halifax, Alice Mahon, to give homeworkers the status of employees. So far she's been unsuccessful but she is not giving up; she plans to present a Bill to the House of Commons in the future which will readdress the homeworking issue.

The problem is homeworkers are scattered, somewhat isolated, and not organised into trade unions . . . and they are predominantly female. Men tend to be more belligerent over employment rights and wages!

When the free European Market arrives in 1992, hopefully it will bring with it help for women who work from home, as legislation in the rest of the EEC is generally better. And as women become an even more vital part of the workforce (it's thought by 1995 they'll be taking four out of five new jobs) and companies start taking their needs a little more seriously (adding childcare to their list of perks) hopefully we'll see improvements in working conditions right across the board – for job sharers, part-timers and homeworkers alike.

Sociologists and authors Carol Wolkowitz and Annie Phizacklea, who have made a study of working from home and analysed our survey, hope some of the myths surrounding homework – that it's an easy option for family life: it's for pin money and so on – will be dispelled. Then, they hope, women will have more leverage when campaigning for a better deal and won't be at such a severe disadvantage just because they need, or want, to work from home.

> "I find it peculiar that my contract says I must work 37 hours if supplied with work, but offers no guarantee I'll be supplied with 37 hours worth – or the money!"
>
> Computer analyst

What can you do?

If you feel strongly about the rights of women working at home, write and tell your local MP, listing the issues you feel should be addressed – like status, salary, rights to holidays, sick pay, etc. And to help Alice Mahon MP in her campaign for protective legislation, send a copy of your letter to her at the House of Commons, Westminster, London SW1A OAA.

Source: *Prima*, September 1990

References

Acker, Joan (1992) 'The future of women and work: ending the twentieth century', *Sociological Perspectives*, 35(1): 53–68.

Albin, Peter and Appelbaum, Eileen (1988) 'The computer rationalisation of work: implications for women workers', in J. Jenson, E. Hagen and C. Reddy (eds), *Feminization of the Labour Force*. Cambridge: Polity Press.

Alexander, S. (1983) *Women's Work in Nineteenth Century London*. London: Journeyman Press.

Allen, Sheila and Wolkowitz, Carol (1986) 'Homeworking and the control of women's labour', *Feminist Review*, 22: 25–51. Reprinted in *Waged Work: a Reader*. London: Virago, 1987.

Allen, Sheila and Wolkowitz, Carol (1987a) *Homeworking: Myths and Realities*. London: Macmillan.

Allen, Sheila and Wolkowitz, Carol (1987b) 'Women's working time'. World Congress of Women, unpublished paper.

Amott, Teresa and Matthaei, Julie (1991) *Race, Gender and Work: a Multicultural Economic History of Women in the United States*. Montreal: Black Rose Books.

Anthias, Floya (1983) 'Sexual divisions and ethnic adaptations: the case of Greek-Cypriot Women', in A. Phizacklea (ed.), *One Way Ticket*. London: Routledge.

Anwar, Shakeel and Chai, Kim-wah (1994) 'Using credit to create jobs', *Europ*, spring, pp. 41–2.

Bagilhole, Barbara (1985) 'The experience of outworking in Nottinghamshire'. Department of Social Administration, University of Nottingham, unpublished paper.

Bakker, Isabella (1988) 'Women's employment in comparative perspective', in J. Jenson, E. Hagen and C. Reddy (eds), *Feminization of the Labour Force*. Cambridge: Polity Press.

Beechey, Veronica and Perkins, Tessa (1987) *A Matter of Hours: Women, Part-time Work and the Labour Market*. Cambridge: Polity Press.

Bell, Daniel (1973) *The Coming of Post-Industrial Society*. New York: Basic Books.

Bella (1990) 'If I stop work the kids will starve', *Bella*, 17 February.

Berk, Sandra (1985) *The Gender Factory*. New York/London: Plenum.

Bhavnani, Reena (1994) *Black Women in the Labour Market: Research Review*. Manchester: Equal Opportunities Commission.

Bisset, L. and Huws, U. (1985) *Sweated Labour: Homeworking in Britain Today*. London: Low Pay Unit, Pamphlet no. 33.

Boden, Rebecca and Corden, Anne (1994) *Measuring Low Incomes: Self-Employment and Family Credit*. London: HMSO, Social Policy Research Unit.

Boris, E. (1989) 'Black women and paid labor in the home: industrial homework in Chicago in the 1920s', in E. Boris and C. Daniels (eds), *Homework: Historical and Contemporary Perspectives on Paid Labor in the Home*. Illinois: University of Illinois Press.

Boris, E. and Daniels, C. (eds) (1989) *Homework: Historical and Contemporary Perspectives on Paid Labor at Home*. Illinois: University of Illinois Press.

Brown, C. (1984) *Black and White Britain: the Third PSI Survey*. London: Heinemann.

Brown, Marie (1974) *Sweated Labour: a Study of Homework*. London: Low Pay Unit, pamphlet no. 1.

Chapkis, Wendy and Enloe, Cynthia (1983) *Of Common Cloth*. Amsterdam: Transnational Institute.

Christensen, K, (1985) *Impacts of Computer-mediated Home-based Work on Women and their Families*. New York: Center for Human Environments.

Christensen, K. (1988a) *Women and Home-based Work: the Unspoken Contract*. New York: Holt.

Christensen, K. (1988b) *Flexible Workstyles: a Look at Contingent Labor*. Washington, DC: US Department of Labor.

Christensen, K. (ed.) (1988c) *The New Era of Home-based Work: Directions and Policies*. Boulder, Colorado: Westview Press.

Christensen, K. (1989) 'Home-based clerical work: no simple truth, no simple reality', in E. Boris and C. Daniels (eds), *Homework: Historical and Contemporary Perspectives on Paid Labour at Home*. Illinois: University of Illinois Press.

Commission for Racial Equality (1982) *Massey Ferguson Perkins Ltd: Report of a Formal Investigation*. London: CRE.

Conference Board (1989) *Flexible Staffing amd Scheduling in US Corporations*. New York: Conference Board, Research Bulletin 240.

Cook, Jacqui (1991) *The Prospects for Home Professional Teleworking*. Aberdeen: BT City Communications Centre.

Cragg, Arnold and Dawson, Tim (1981) *Qualitative Research among Homeworkers*, Research paper no. 21. London: Department of Employment.

Crine, Simon (1979) *The Hidden Army*. London: Low Pay Unit.

Crompton, Rosemary and Sanderson, Kay (1990) *Gendered Jobs and Social Change*. London: Unwin Hyman.

Dangler, J. (1989) 'Electronic sub-assemblers in New York', in E. Boris and C. Daniels (eds), *Homework: Historical and Comparative Perspectives on Paid Labor in the Home*. Illinois: University of Illinois Press.

Daniels, C. (1989) 'Between home and factory: homeworkers and the state', in E. Boris and C. Daniels (eds), *Homework: Historical and Contemporary Perspectives on Paid Labor in the Home*. Illinois: University of Illinois Press.

Department of Employment (1987) 'Ethnic origin and economic status', *Employment Gazette*, pp. 18–29, January.

Dex, S. and Shaw, L.B. (1986) *British and American Women at Work*. Basingstoke: Macmillan.

Dobash, R. and Dobash, R. (1992) *Women, Violence and Social Change*. London: Routledge.

Elias, P. and Gregory, M. (1992) *The Changing Structure of Occupations and Earnings in Great Britain, 1975–1990*. Coventry: Institute for Employment Research, University of Warwick.

Eurostat (1989) Brussels: Commission for European Communities, Statistical Office.

Fraser, L. and Gordon, L. (1994) 'A genealogy of dependency', *Signs*, 19(2), winter.

Gaffikin, F.A. and Nickson, A. (n.d.) *Jobs Crisis and the Multi-nationals: the Case of the West Midlands*. Birmingham: Trade Union Resource Centre.

Garrett, M. (1984) *Homeworking in Southwark*. London: Southwark Employment Unit.

Glyn, Andrew and Miliband, David (eds) (1994) *Paying for Inequality: the Social Cost of Social Injustice*. London: IPPR/Rivers Oram Press.

Gordon, G. (1988) 'The dilemmas of telework: technology versus tradition', in W. Korte, W. Steinle and S. Robinson (eds), *Telework*. Amsterdam: North-Holland.

Gorz, André (1985) *Paths to Paradise*. London: Pluto Press.

Government Statistical Service (1989) *New Earnings Survey 1989*, Parts E and F. Department of Employment. London: HMSO.

Greater London Council (1986) *The London Labour Plan*. London: GLC.

Greater Manchester Low Pay Unit (1986) *Homeworking: a Report on Homeworking Prepared for Manchester City Council*. Manchester Low Pay Unit, Economic Briefing Note no. 62.

Greater Manchester Low Pay Unit (n.d.) *Working at Home*. Manchester.

Haddon, Leslie and Silverstone, Roger (1993) *Teleworking in the 1990s: a View from Home*. Brighton: SPRU CICT Report Series, no. 10.

Hakim, C. (1980) 'Homeworking: some new evidence', *Employment Gazette*, 80(10), 1105–9.

Hakim, C. (1984) 'Homework and outwork: national estimates from two surveys', *Employment Gazette*, 92: 7–12.

Hakim, C. (1987a) 'Homeworking in Britain: key findings from the National Survey of Home-based Workers', *Employment Gazette*, 95: 92–104.

Hakim, C. (1987b) *Home-based Work in Britain: a Report on the 1981 Homeworking Survey*. London: Department of Employment Research Paper no. 60.

Hakim, C. (1988) 'Self-employment in Britain: a review of recent trends and current issues', *Work, Employment and Society*, 2(4), December.

Hakim, C. (1991) 'Grateful slaves and self-made women: fact and fantasy in women's work orientations', *European Sociological Review*, 7(2), September.

Harding, S. (ed.) (1987) *Feminism and Methodology*. Milton Keynes: Open University Press.

Heath, A. (1981) *Social Mobility*. London: Fontana.

Hewitt, P. (1993) *About Time: the Revolution in Work and Family Life*. London: IPPR/Rivers Oram Press.

Huws, Ursula (1984) *The New Homeworkers: New Technology and the Changing Location of White-collar Work*, pamphlet no. 28. London: Low Pay Unit.

Huws, Ursula, Korte, Verner and Robinson, Simon (1990) *Telework: Towards the Elusive Office*. Chichester: Wiley.

Independent on Sunday (1992) 'A flexible approach to teleworking is changing the way offices are managed', 17 May.

Independent on Sunday (1993) 'The New Ruralists', 25 April, pp. 68–71.

IRS Employment Trends (1989) 'Telework campaign will relocate high-tech jobs', 438, 25 April, p. 4.

IRS Employment Trends (1991a) 'Civil service issues: homeworking guidelines', 481, 8 February, pp. 2–3.

IRS Employment Trends (1991b) 'Teleworking increases productivity', 486, 26 April, p. 5.

IRS Employment Trends (1991c) 'Homeworking agreement concluded at IBM', 498, 18 October, p. 15.

Jenson, Jane, Hagen, Elisabeth and Reddy, Ceallaigh (eds) (1988) *Feminization of the Labour Force*. Cambridge: Polity Press.

Keat, Russell and Abercrombie, Nicholas (eds) (1991) *Enterprise Culture*. London: Routledge.

Leat, Diana and Gay, Pat (1987) *Paying for Care: a Study of Policy and Practice in Paid Care Schemes*. London: Policy Studies Institute.

Leighton, Patricia and Felstead, Alan (eds) (1992) *The New Entrepreneurs: Self-Employment and Small Business in Europe.* London: Kogan Page.

Liff, Sonia (1993) 'From equality to diversity', paper given at the Conference on Organisations, Gender and Power, University of Warwick Industrial Relations Unit, 15 December.

Lyotard, J.F. (1984) *The Postmodern Condition.* Manchester: Manchester University Press.

McCrudden, C., Smith, D. and Brown, C. (1991) *Racial Justice at Work.* London: Policy Studies Institute.

Maguire, P. (1987) *Doing Participatory Research: a Feminist Approach.* Amherst, MA: Centre for International Education.

Manchester School of Management (1994) *Bulletin on Women and Employment in the EU,* no. 4, April.

Marsden, P., Kalleberg, A.L. and Cook, C.R. (1993) 'Gender differences in organisational commitment: influences of work position and family roles', *Work and Occupations,* 20(3): 368–90.

Mitter, S. (1986a) 'Industrial restructuring and manufacturing homework: immigrant women in the clothing industry', *Capital and Class,* 27: 37–80.

Mitter, S. (1986b) *Common Fate, Common Bond.* London: Pluto Press.

Mitter, S. (1994) 'On organising women in casualised work: a global review', in S. Rowbotham and S. Mitter (eds), *Dignity and Daily Bread.* London/New York: Routledge.

Mitter, S., Phizacklea, A., Totterdill, P. and Wolkowitz, C. (1993) 'Tower Hamlets Homeworkers Co-operative Project Report', unpublished.

Morokvasic, M., Phizacklea, A. and Rudolf, H. (1986) 'Small firms and minority groups: contradictory trends in the French, German and British clothing industries', *International Sociology,* 1: 397–420.

National Group on Homeworking (1994) 'Home truths: key results from the NHG National Homeworking Survey', draft report.

Oakley, Ann (1974) *The Sociology of Housework.* New York: Pantheon Books.

Oakley, Ann (1981) 'Interviewing women: a contradiction in terms', in H. Roberts (ed.), *Doing Feminist Research.* London: Routledge.

Office of Population, Censuses and Surveys (1990) *Standard Occupational Classifications.* London: HMSO.

Olson, M. (1989) 'Organisation barriers to professional telework', in E. Boris and C. Daniels (eds), *Homework: Historical and Contemporary Perspectives on Paid Labor in the Home.* Illinois: University of Illinois Press.

Owen, David (1994) *Ethnic Minority Women and the Labour Market: an Analysis of the 1991 Census.* Manchester: Equal Opportunities Commission.

Pahl, Jan (1985) *Private Violence and Public Policy.* London: Routledge.

Pennington, S. and Westover, B. (1989) *A Hidden Workforce.* London: Macmillan.

Phizacklea, Annie (1983) *One-Way Ticket.* London: Routledge.

Phizacklea, Annie (1988) 'Gender, racism and occupational segregation', in S. Walby (ed.), *Gender Segregation at Work.* Milton Keynes: Open University Press.

Phizacklea, Annie (1990) *Unpacking the Fashion Industry: Gender, Racism and Class in Production.* London: Routledge.

Phizacklea, Annie (1994) 'A single or a segregated market? gendered and racialized divisions', in Haleh Afshar and Mary Maynard (eds), *The Dynamics of 'Race' and Gender: Some Feminist Interventions.* London: Taylor and Francis.

Pollert, Anna (1988) 'The "Flexible Firm": Fixation or Fact', *Work, Employment and Society,* 2(3): 281–316.

Porter Benson, S. (1989) 'Women, work and the family', in E. Boris and C. Daniels (eds), *Homework: Historical and Contemporary Perspectives on Paid Labor in the Home.* Illinois: University of Illinois Press.

Power, M. (1988) 'Women, the state and the family in the US: Reaganomics and the experience of women', in Jill Rubery (ed.), *Women and Recession.* London: Routledge.

Probert, B. and Wajcman, J. (1988) 'Technological change and the future of work', *Journal of Industrial Relations,* September.

Prugl, E. (1990) 'Defining homework: a postscript to the Netherlands Conference on Homework'. Paper presented to the Fourth International Inter-disciplinary Congress on Women, Hunter College, New York.

Rai, K. and Sheikh, N. (1989) *Homeworking.* Birmingham: National Unit on Homeworking.

Reskin, Barbara and Padavic, Irene (1994) *Women and Men at Work.* Thousand Oaks, CA: Pine Forge Press.

Roberts, Bethan (1994) *Minority Ethnic Women: Work, Unemployment and Education.* Manchester: Equal Opportunities Commission.

Rowbotham, Sheila (1993) *Homeworkers Worldwide.* London: Merlin Press.

Rowbotham, S. (1994) 'Strategies against sweated work in Britain, 1820–1920', in S. Rowbotham and S. Mitter (eds), *Dignity and Daily Bread.* London/New York: Routledge.

Rowbotham, Sheila and Mitter, S. (eds) (1994) *Dignity and Daily Bread: New Forms of Economic Organising among Poor Women in the Third World and the First.* London: Routledge.

Roxby, B.C. (1984) *The Forgotten Workers: a Study of the Legal Problems Faced by Homeworkers.* Leicester: Leicester Outwork Campaign.

Rubery, Jill (1988) 'Women and recession: a comparative perspective', in Jill Rubery (ed.), *Women and Recession*. London: Routledge and Kegan Paul.

Scott, Joan (1988) *Gender and the Politics of History*. New York: Columbia University Press.

Silver, H. (1989) 'The demand for homework: evidence from the US Census', in E. Boris and C. Daniels (eds), *Homework: Historical and Contemporary Perspectives on Paid Labor in the Home*. Illinois: University of Illinois Press.

Smith, Dorothy (1987) *The Everyday World as Problematic: a Feminist Sociology*. Milton Keynes: Open University Press.

Tate, J. (1993) *Homeworking in the EC: Report of the ad hoc Working Group*. Brussels: European Commission, Employment, Industrial Relations and Social Affairs, Doc. V/7173/93-EN.

Tate, J. (1994) 'Homework in West Yorkshire', in S. Rowbotham and S. Mitter (eds), *Dignity and Daily Bread*. London/New York: Routledge.

Toffler, A. (1981) *The Third Wave*. London: Collins/Pan.

Wakewich, Pamela (1989) 'Greek women and broken nerves in Montreal', *Medical Anthropology*, 11(1): 29–45.

Westwood, S. and Bhachu, P. (ed.) (1988) *Enterprising Women: Ethnicity, Economy and Gender Relations*. London: Routledge.

West Yorkshire Homeworking Group (1990) *A Penny a Bag: Campaigning on Homework*. Batley: Yorkshire and Humberside Low Pay Unit.

Wolverhampton Homeworkers Research Project (1984) *Report*. Wolverhampton: Wolverhampton Trades Council.

Woody, Bette (1992) *Black Women in the Workplace: Impacts of Structural Change in the Economy*. New York: Greenwood Press.

Working for Childcare (1991) *A Working Choice for Parents: the Case for a National Childcare Strategy*. London: Working for Childcare.

Index